D0668627

# Simple
# Sermons
# for
# 20th century
# Christians

THE "SIMPLE SERMON" SERIES BY W. HERSCHEL FORD . . .

*Seven Simple Sermons on the Saviour's Last Words*
*Seven Simple Sermons on the Second Coming*
*Simple Sermons About Jesus Christ*
*Simple Sermons for a Sinful Age*
*Simple Sermons for Funeral Services*
*Simple Sermons for Midweek Services*
*Simple Sermons for Saints and Sinners*
*Simple Sermons for Special Days and Occasions*
*Simple Sermons for Sunday Evening*
*Simple Sermons for Sunday Morning*
*Simple Sermons for Time and Eternity*
*Simple Sermons for Times Like These*
*Simple Sermons for Today's World*
*Simple Sermons for 20th Century Christians*
*Simple Sermons on Conversion and Commitment*
*Simple Sermons From the Book of Acts*
*Simple Sermons From the Gospel of John*
*Simple Sermons From the Gospel of Matthew*
*Simple Sermons on Evangelistic Themes*
*Simple Sermons on Heaven, Hell and Judgment*
*Simple Sermons on Prayer*
*Simple Sermons on Prophetic Themes*
*Simple Sermons on Salvation and Service*
*Simple Sermons on Simple Themes*
*Simple Sermons on the Christian Life*
*Simple Sermons on Great Christian Doctrines*
*Simple Sermons on the Old-Time Religion*
*Simple Sermons on the Seven Churches of Revelation*
*Simple Sermons on the Ten Commandments*
*Simple Talks for Christian Workers*
*Simple Sermons on Life and Living*
*Simple Sermons for Modern Man*
*Simple Sermons on Old Testament Texts*
*Simple Sermons on New Testament Texts*

# Simple Sermons for 20th century Christians

by

W. HERSCHEL FORD, D.D.

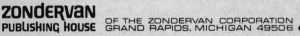

ZONDERVAN
PUBLISHING HOUSE

OF THE ZONDERVAN CORPORATION
GRAND RAPIDS, MICHIGAN 49506

*This book is*
*affectionately dedicated*
*to*
Dr. Jess C. Moody
*of West Palm Beach, Florida*
*beloved friend,*

*dynamic gospel preacher,*
*warm-hearted pastor,*
*and*
*his charming and*
*wonderful wife,* Doris

# Foreword

A few days ago I received a letter from a preacher in Korea. He said that another preacher had preached one of my *Simple Sermons* and that four souls had been saved. Now that's good news indeed. I receive many such letters.

That is why these books have been written and published. This is the twenty-third volume in the *Simple Sermon Series*. May God bless all those who read and use these messages for the glory of God and the salvation of souls.

Preachers and Christian workers are certainly free to use these messages or any part of them as their very own.

*4719-D Skillman Street*
*Dallas, Texas 75206*

W. HERSCHEL FORD

# CONTENTS

# Simple
# Sermons
# for
# 20th century
# Christians

# 1.

# The Children of God

## John 1:12

Who are the children of God? Today many people who haven't studied the Bible glibly talk about "the Fatherhood of God." They declare that every person in the world is a child of God. Now the Bible doesn't teach that. It plainly tells us that some people are the children of the devil. It also plainly tells us how to become children of God. It is true that all of us are creatures of God. He created us, but that doesn't make us His children. He created the cows and the horses, but they are not His children.

In John 8:44 we hear Jesus talking to a group of unbelievers. He tells them that they are children of the devil. But in John 1:12 we read that "as many as received him, to them gave he power to become the sons of God." Now if every one is already a child of God, it would not be necessary for them to do something to become children of God. So the Bible tells us that we become children of God by receiving Jesus Christ as our Saviour.

In this chapter I would like for you to look with me at some of the characteristics of a child of God. We will use the letter "S" in picking out these characteristics.

## I. A Child of God Is a Saved Person

When he came into the world he was lost. If he had continued on that course of sin he would still be on the way to eternal death. But something has happened to him. He has met Christ; He has had a personal experience with Him. He has repented of his sins and trusted Christ for time and eternity. One night when Jesus rested from the weary labors of the day a prominent man came to see Him. He was Nicodemus, a

man of position and power and a member of the Sanhedrin. But
he was not happy. Life held no joy and no peace for him. He
was reaching out for something that satisfied but could not
find it. Then he heard some wonderful things about Jesus. So
when Nicodemus learned that Jesus was in town he slipped out
to see Him under the cover of darkness and poured out his
heart to the Saviour. Jesus looked deep into that heart and
said to him, "Nicodemus, you must be born again. You cannot
see the kingdom of God unless you have been born again."

As you follow the conversation in John 3 you learn how
to be born again. We read, "As Moses lifted up the serpent in
the wilderness, even so must the Son of Man be lifted up;
That whosoever believeth in him should not perish, but have
eternal life" (verses 14, 15). Then we read those wonderful
words in the sixteenth verse, "For God so loved the world,
that he gave his only begotten Son, that whosoever believeth
in him should not perish, but have everlasting life." Jesus continues in verse 18, "He that believeth on him is not condemned;
but he that believeth not is condemned already, because he hath
not believed in the name of the only begotten Son of God."
You see then that a man is born again when he puts his faith
in the Lord Jesus Christ. The child of God has done that,
therefore he is saved.

Paul and Silas sang and prayed in the jail at Philippi. God
sent an earthquake to shake the world and the prisoners were
released from their bonds. The Philippian jailer, falling before
them, cried out, "What must I do to be saved?" And Paul
answered, "Believe on the Lord Jesus Christ and thou shalt be
saved" (Acts 16:30, 31). The child of God has done that,
therefore he is saved.

As a saved man the child of God is a different man. A
man in Springfield, Missouri, was a cursing, whiskey-drinking,
unconverted church member. He was in the feed business. A
good Christian man came and bought feed for his cattle from
this feed man so that he could talk to him about his soul. Instead
of buying enough feed for a week, he bought enough just for
one day at a time so that he could have an extra opportunity
to talk to this lost soul. The man who owned the store wanted

the business, so he let the Christian man come every day for three months and talk to him. Finally the lost man became so convicted of his sin that he went down into the basement of his store at five o'clock in the morning, fell upon his knees and prayed, "Lord, I can't promise you anything. I promised my wife that I would quit drinking and quit cursing, but I couldn't quit. However, my friend tells me that You can give a man a new heart. I certainly need one. This old heart of mine is just full of sin. Please give me a new heart." Three days later he mashed his finger and had to go to the doctor to get it dressed. Then he thought of something and said to himself, "I haven't cursed in three days." God saved him and gave him a new heart. All the drinking and cursing became a thing of the past. He became a new man in Christ Jesus.

Yes, the child of God is a saved person, and a saved person is a changed person.

## II. A Child of God Is a Separated Person

We ought to be able to see a great difference in a man after he has been saved. Christians ought to be different from the rest of the world. Why is it that the church doesn't have the power today that it ought to have? It is because our church members are not separated from the world. You can't tell them from anyone else. They go to the same places that the sinners do, they do the same things, they talk the same way. But the world will never know that we belong to Christ until they can see a difference in our lives.

Jesus told us that we are to be "in the world, but not of the world." Walking along one day He pointed to a lily and said, "Solomon in all his glory was not arrayed like one of these" (Matthew 6:29). I have seen a lily growing in the muck and mire of the swamp, but it lifted up its head above its environment and shone forth in all the glory and beauty of that wonderful flower. It must be that way with Christians. They must lift up their heads and their hearts and lives above the world. A man said to Mr. Moody, "Now that I am converted, do I have to give up the world?" And Mr. Moody answered,

"No, you give a ringing testimony for Christ and the world will give you up. They will not want you."

When we speak of living a separated life some people think that this means not dancing or playing cards or going to shows. They don't do these things, so they boast of their separation. But I tell you that it goes down deeper than that. It means not only physical separation, but spiritual separation. I am thinking now of a couple who were formerly members of our church. If I blasted any worldly practice or spoke of separation in a sermon they would come up and compliment me. Yet they showed a mean and ugly spirit in their own lives. Separation is more than physical, it is spiritual. A child of God lives a separated life.

### III. The Child of God Is a Settled Person

1. *He is settled as to his church membership.* He doesn't say, "I have been born again and that is enough." He says, "Christ has saved me, therefore I will go into His church and go to work for Him." Now that church is not to be selected on the basis of its location or its ritual or its friendliness. The saved person ought to take the Bible and study the beliefs and practices of the New Testament church, then he ought to join the church which comes nearest to that pattern.

2. *He is settled in his convictions.* He gains these convictions in three ways: by reading the Bible, through prayer, and by following the guidance of the Holy Spirit.

> Dare to be a Daniel,
> Dare to stand alone,
> Dare to have a purpose firm,
> Dare to make it known.

3. *He is settled as to his contributions.* When you learn to practice God's way of giving, you don't have to worry about the matter any more. Just give God His tithe and if possible an offering over and above. Then everything is settled. You see then that the child of God is settled as to his church, his convictions and his contributions.

### IV. THE CHILD OF GOD IS A SINCERE PERSON

This simply means that what he says is true. It comes from his heart. There is no mixture of hypocrisy in it. In my first pastorate a deacon who was well up in years and who had served for a long time asked me to take him off the board, so that some younger man could serve in his place. I did this, thinking that he was sincere in what he asked. But after this was done he would have very little to do with the church. He said that it was a shame for him to be taken off the board after he had served faithfully for so many years. Every pastor has had many experiences like this.

### V. THE CHILD OF GOD IS A SWEET PERSON

Are you surprised that I should say this? I have said that he is saved, separated, settled and sincere. I believe that he ought to be sweet also. Some people are fine church members. They attend church regularly, they serve in some position, they pay their tithe. But they lack that sweetness of spirit which Jesus had and which they ought to have. When people described the Christians of the first century, what did they say about them? We read, "They took note of them, that they had been with Jesus" (Acts 4:13). Now if you are grouchy and irritable are you ever going to make someone else think of Jesus? Of course not.

On the inside of the dome of the national capitol a number of angels are painted. When the artist first painted these angels the committee said to him, "Your form and color are all right, but the faces of the angels lack spirituality." He painted the angels again and again he received the same criticism. Finally it began to dawn on him that in order to get spirituality into the faces of the angels he must first have it in his own heart. He sought the Lord with all of his heart and God saved him. He became a new man in Christ Jesus. Only then could he put spirituality into the faces of the angels. And the only way we can be the sweet Christians we ought to be is by having the spirit of Christ in our hearts. We must live very close to Him and learn to love all for whom He died.

Let me show you a Bible character who grew sweeter as the years went by. John the Apostle, when he was a young man, was called a "son of thunder" (Mark 3:17). One day a certain city was unkind to Jesus and John said, "Lord, let's burn up the city and everything in it." That's the kind of disposition he had. But he lived about seventy more years after that in close fellowship with Jesus. Now listen to the old man. All that he can talk about is love. And instead of wanting to burn people, we hear him calling them "my little children" (I John 2:1). Yes, it takes a close walk with Jesus to make us sweet.

## VI. The Child of God Is a Steadfast Person

Here is a good motto for a Christian, "Therefore, my beloved brethren, be ye stedfast, unmoveable, always abounding in the work of the Lord, forasmuch as ye know that your labour is not in vain in the Lord" (I Corinthians 15:58). This means from the moment that you are saved until you meet Jesus in heaven or in the air you are to be true and faithful in all spiritual matters.

1. *The child of God is to be steadfast in prayer.* How much do you pray? Do you live in an atmosphere of prayer or do you just pray when you get in trouble? Phillips Brooks said, "Prayer is a wish turned heavenward."

The Westminster Catechism says that "prayer is an offering up of our desires unto God, for things agreeable to His will, in the Name of Christ, with confession of our sins, and with thankful acknowledgement of all of His mercies."

2. *The child of God is to be steadfast in studying God's Word.* The child of God ought to love to read the Father's love letter, for that is what the Bible is. A great Christian said, "Apply thyself wholly to the Scriptures and apply the Scriptures wholly to thyself." Now some people do the first thing. They read the Bible faithfully, but they don't do the second thing. They don't apply Bible truth to themselves. I talked to an old man in North Carolina who told me that he and his wife read the Bible every day. Yet they were not Christians. They had never seen from the Bible that they

were lost sinners needing a Saviour. If you read the Bible in the light of your own needs, it will indeed become a source of great strength and help.

3. *The child of God is to be steadfast in service.* Someone has said that service is the rent which we pay for the space we occupy on earth. But if every second of every minute of every hour of every day of every week of every month of every year we spent on earth were spent in serving Christ who saved us, we could never pay for Calvary and salvation.

Some of our church members remind me of a letter of recommendation written by a certain man. Another man wanted a gardener and asked this man to write him a recommendation of John Smith. And here is what the man wrote, "John Smith has an excellent knowledge of gardening. He knows about the chemistry of the soil. He knows just what and when to plant. He knows how to cultivate the finest flowers and make a garden a thing of beauty." When the man read this letter he said, "Why that is just the man I want." Then he noticed three words at the bottom of the page that ruined everything. The other man had written, "But he won't."

We have hundreds of church members who could do a mighty work for the Lord. The trouble is that they won't. They are either too lazy, too indifferent, too worldly, or too disinterested. But the child of God ought to be steadfast.

## VII. The Child of God Is a Safe Person

Waves of trouble may sweep over his soul. Temptations may beset him on every side. Death may come, but he is safe — safe for heaven. You and I are not very much or very good or very strong. But Christ is such a great Saviour that He saves forever. The minute after you trust Christ you are just as safe for heaven as if you were already there.

A preacher friend of mine was a chaplain in World War II. He went through many hardships, and rejoiced greatly when the war was over. He boarded a plane in France and immediately went to sleep. When he woke up he was back in America. When a Christian goes to sleep in death, he is safe in the arms of Jesus and he wakes up in heaven.

Are you a child of God? If not, you can become a child of God now through faith in the Lord Jesus Christ. Tomorrow could be too late.

A Christian from Chicago was going to Houston. He had a stopover of two hours in Dallas, so he went to see a friend who was quite sick. He urged the friend to receive Christ, but the man said, "No, come back to see me on your return trip, and I will settle the matter." "But you are a very sick man," said the Christian, "why not take my Saviour now?" "Oh," said the man, "I will be all right in a few days." The Christian man saw that he could do nothing for his friend, so he continued his journey. When he arrived in Houston he received a telegram saying, "He died five minutes after you left." It could happen to you. "As many as received him, to them gave he power to become the sons of God." Will you receive Him?

## 2.

# That's Why I Love Jesus

John 21:15-17

This is a personal sermon. In it I want to tell you why I love Jesus. My only object is to glorify His precious Name and to try to get you to fall in love with Him, too. "The proof of the pudding is in the eating." I have tasted of the Lord Jesus Christ and found Him sweeter than honey in the comb. I want to share Him with you.

I feel very much like a little boy I read about years ago. The daughter of a Chicago millionaire was paralyzed. The American doctors could not help her, so her father wrote out a check for $20,000 and sent it to the famous Dr. Lorenz of Vienna, pleading with him to come to America and to minister to his little girl. The great doctor did come and did help the millionaire's daughter. But in a poor section of the city there lived a very poor family. In this family there was a little fourteen-year-old boy who suffered from the same affliction as the rich man's daughter. The family was too poor to afford a doctor or buy a wheelchair.

When this little boy saw Dr. Lorenz' picture in the paper and read about what he had done for the little girl, he said, "Mother, wouldn't it be wonderful if the doctor could make me walk?" The mother's heart broke as she said, "Honey, that rich man paid $20,000 for Dr. Lorenz' service and we don't have a cent." "Well," said the boy, "a guy can wish, can't he, mother?" The mother fled into another room to weep.

Then it seemed that God was putting an idea into her mind. She went down to the hotel and knocked on the door of the doctor's suite. When Dr. Lorenz opened the door she fell on her knees before him and sobbed out her story. The doctor asked, "Madam, do you have any money?" "No," she

19

answered. "Then I will operate on your boy free of charge." The poor woman was so grateful that she began to kiss the doctor's feet and he had to restrain her.

Well, the doctor had the boy taken to a good hospital. The operation was performed and the boy was kept in the hospital eleven weeks. One morning when his mother came into the room, the boy said, "Mother, go and look out the window." "Why, son?" she asked. "Never mind," said the boy, "just go and look out the window." The mother went over to the window and stood there a few seconds, then she felt a tug at her sleeve. She turned around, and there was her boy. He had walked for the first time. She hugged him and kissed him and wept for joy.

A few days later Dr. Lorenz came in and said, "You are all right now, son. Go home and be a good boy." The boy caught the doctor's hand and kissed it. The doctor said, "Don't do that," and the boy shouted, "Doctor, as long as there is a tongue in my head, ain't nobody going to hear the last of what you did for me."

Jesus did far more for me than that doctor did for that poor boy. I am the only one who knows how much He did. And I can never tell all of it.

I.   I Love Him for What He Has Done
II.  I Love Him for What He Is Doing Now
III. I Love Him for What He Is Going to Do

## I.  I Love Him for What He Has Done

What did He do?

1. *He loved me while I was a sinner.* All sin is rebellion against God. I had rebelled, I had sinned, yet He loved me. Romans 5:8 says, "But God commendeth his love toward us, in that while we were yet sinners, Christ died for us."

Just think of it! A king has certain subjects. They rebel against him, they take up arms against him. They seek to depose him, yet he cares for them enough to die for them. Wouldn't that be strange behavior for a king? Well, the sinner rebels against Christ. He says, "I will not have this Man to rule over me. I will go my own way, regardless. I despise His law. I reject His authority." Yet, in spite of all this, Jesus still loves us. He looked down from heaven and loved even me, although I had sinned against Him. No wonder I love Him.

2. *He paid the price for my sin.* Some time ago I held a revival in a small town and stayed in the pastor's home. He had two fine children, a boy and a girl, and I fell in love with them. One afternoon the boy found a cigarette and took it to his room, lit it, and began to puff on it. His mother smelled the smoke, ran to the room and caught the boy in the act. When his father came in, the mother told him about it and he said to the boy, "I'll punish you later." That night in the church service God spoke to the boy's heart. He came to the front and said, "God has called me to be a preacher and I am surrendering my life to Him."

When we reached home after that glorious service I said to the father, "You're not going to whip him now, are you?" And that wise preacher-father said, "Yes, he was disobedient. I am going to keep my promise." I loved the boy and wanted to take his place, but I could not. Listen, I had sinned and hell's punishment was awaiting me. But Jesus went to the Father and said, "I love that poor sinner. Let Me take his place." And Christ went all the way to Calvary and died in my stead. No wonder I love Him.

3. *He sent the Holy Spirit to convict me and point me to Christ.* When He went back to heaven He said He would send the Holy Spirit to take His place on the earth. Jesus is not here now in person, but the Holy Spirit is here, doing His work. A sinner comes to church. Christ doesn't tap him on the shoulder and show him his need and the way of salvation. But the Holy Spirit does just that.

He certainly convicted me as I sat in the balcony and looked down upon the service going on below me. I felt mean and low and lost and helpless and hopeless. But then He gave me hope. The Holy Spirit said: "Look up, sinner, there is hope for you." And I looked, oh, yes, I looked. I saw an old rugged cross. I saw the Lamb of God dying on that cross. I knew He was taking my place. I heard Him inviting me to Him. My heart bounded with joy. I knew I would not forever suffer in hell. He had paid the full price for me on Calvary.

Wounded for me, wounded for me,
There on the cross He was wounded for me;
Gone my transgressions, and now I am free,
All because Jesus was wounded for me.

Dying for me, dying for me,
There on the cross He was dying for me;
Now in His death my redemption I see,
All because Jesus was dying for me.

Coming for me, coming for me,
One day to earth He is coming for me;
Then with what joy His dear face I shall see,
Oh, how I praise Him! He's coming for me.

4. *He saved me, wrote my name in the Lamb's book of life and gave me eternal life.* One day, when Jesus was here, He said, "Him that cometh to me I will in no wise cast out" (John 6:37). When I came to Him He didn't rebuke me, He didn't scold me, He just took me in His arms, dried my tears, and saved me. He said He would forgive my sins and He did. He said He would take me into His family and He did. "As many as received him, to them gave he power to become the sons of God" (John 1:12). He said He would write my name on high and He did. He said He would give me everlasting life and He did.

Some years ago I visited Silver Springs, Florida, for the first time. I signed my name in a guest book which contained thousands of other names. That was not important. The thing that is important is that my name is written in His book, and no power in earth or heaven or hell can erase it. Yes, He saved me.

5. *He called me to preach the Gospel.* Years ago I was a member of a young peoples' group in our church. Often when I would make a little talk, someone would say, "You ought to be a preacher." But I said, "No, that is not for me." Of course I didn't know then what God had in mind for me. Then, one glorious June morning in a great sunrise service, the Lord spoke to me in a voice almost as audible as the voice I am using right

now. He said to me, "If you love Me I want you to turn your back upon every earthly ambition and desire and give your life to me as a gospel preacher." And that morning I made my surrender of life and talents to Him. Now after more than forty years in the ministry, my only regret is that I haven't served Him in a better manner. I have heard preachers say that they entered the ministry because they, in themselves, felt that this was the way they could best serve God. It was not so with me. I entered the ministry because of a clear and definite call from the Lord.

A young man in New York was offered a job in Boston and was packing to leave. His mother said, "Son, there is a picture in a department store that I want you to see." The young man pled that he didn't have time to do this. Then his mother said as she put her arms around him, "Son, you'll soon be gone. I won't be able to ask you for any more favors. Please do this for me." "All right," he said, "if you put it that way." She took him down to the store and pushed open the door of a certain room. There in the darkened room under a shaft of light he saw a man on his knees, praying. He moved a little closer and saw that it was a picture. So wonderful and so beautiful was the picture that his heart was touched and stirred. He didn't enjoy the party he attended that night. He couldn't get the picture out of his mind.

The next day he said, "Mother, let's go and see that picture again." They went to the store and into the room and he looked at the picture for a long time. Then he said, "Mother, why is He so sad? Why are His hands so pleading?" She answered, "Son, that's Jesus praying in Gethsemane. He is thinking of those for whom He is going to die. He is thinking of the multitudes who will need to know of His death. He is praying for God to raise up men and women to tell His story." The young man bowed his head and said, "Blessed Lord, if anything is left undone that I can do, you can count on me."

That's the way I felt. And over the years He has led and blessed me. He helped me to finish high school, college and seminary after I was married and had two children. I love Him and praise Him for all He has done. I couldn't have pastored a church or held a revival or preached a sermon or written a book without His help.

Yes, I love Him for what He has done for me in the past. You may not have had my experience. You may not be called to preach the Gospel. But the Lord has some work for you to do. He needs your help.

## II.  I Love Him for What He Is Doing Now

1. *He is daily forgiving my sins.* When we are saved we are not made perfect. We still have that old carnal nature. Satan still tempts us and we often fall into his net. This hurts Jesus, but in His love He says: "If you will confess your sins, God is faithful and just to forgive and cleanse." Yes, I can go to Him in penitence and confession and He forgives me. Then I can sing, "Nothing between my soul and the Saviour." Oh, it's a grand and glorious feeling.

Once God had a wonderful servant, David. He called him, "a man after my own heart." David wrote such wonderful things as "the Lord is my shepherd" and "God is my refuge." He was a great man of God. He never did anything by halves. So one day he committed a great sin, but God would not let him get away with it. He sent Nathan to say, "Thou art the man, thou hast sinned." And David, deeply convicted, fell before God and cried out, "I have sinned." After his confession Nathan said to him, "The Lord also has put away your sin." David then wrote the 32nd Psalm, saying, "My heart was heavy night and day. I wept over my sin. But God forgave me and now I am the happiest man in the world."

I, too, have sinned often. I have felt the weight of my sin. I have wept out my confession to God. And I have heard Him say, "I forgive you, my child." And He put a song in my heart.

2. *He is helping me to live.* We are in a hard world. We can't go on in our own strength. We need outside help, the help that God alone can give. A little girl was walking down the street with her father. When they started to cross the street the father offered his hand to the little girl, but she refused to take it. She felt that she could get along by herself. But when

she saw the cars roaring down the street, she reached up for her father's strong hand.

Often we think we can get along by ourselves, but when life presses in upon us, we are wise to reach up for the nail-pierced hands of Jesus. He alone can help us over the rugged ways of our pilgrim journey.

3. *He is comforting me.* I know what sorrow is. I know something of the heartbreaks of life. But I know something else. I am not alone. The Holy Spirit is the God who "walks along beside us." So in sorrow I call on Him and He comforts me.

4. *He is answering my prayers.* Do you doubt that God answers prayer? Then you have never really and truly prayed. The Bible is full of prayer promises. If you claim these promises, God always makes good.

I have been in revivals where I had to preach twice daily. Often I would be sick, I would be aching all over, I would be hoarse and weak. But I have prayed earnestly. Then as I stood up to preach the pain disappeared and God helped me to preach. He had answered my prayers. And every one who prays can say, "Here is where He answered me and here is another place where He answered."

### III. I Love Him for What He Is Going to Do

1. *First, He will come back for me.* He said, "I go to prepare a place for you. And if I go and prepare a place for you, I will come again, and receive you unto myself; that where I am, there ye may be also" (John 14:2, 3). He will come in one of two ways.

He may come in death. If the Lord tarries I know I shall die. What does that mean for a Christian? It means that his body will be placed in a grave, but his soul will go up to be with Jesus. "Absent from the body, present with the Lord" (II Corinthians 5:8). Then when He comes the body will be raised, spirit and body will be joined and salvation will be complete.

But Jesus may come in the air while I am still living. Then the Bible tells us that all Christians will be "caught up . . . to meet the Lord in the air" (I Thessalonians 4:17). Tribulation

is coming upon the earth and Jesus wants to get His children
safely out of the world. Here is a family living in the city. The
father knows that an epidemic is coming, so he takes the family
away to a healthy climate where they will be safe. So Jesus,
knowing of the troubles that are to come upon the earth, takes
His children up to be with Him. Oh, you can't help but love
Him for that!

2. *Then He will transform me and make me like Himself.*
He will do this when He takes me up to be with Him. He
will do it in "the twinkling of an eye" (I Corinthians 15:52).
Oh, what a miracle! Oh, what a Saviour! I wish that I were
more like Him now, but I fall so far short. But when He comes
He will make me like Himself. Philippians 3:21 — "Who shall
change our vile body, that it may be fashioned like unto his
glorious body, according to the working whereby he is able
even to subdue all things unto himself."

3. *Then He will re-unite me with my loved ones.* My
mother died when I was four years of age. It will be a blessed
privilege to see her again. I remember how my father would
sit on the front porch, awaiting my arrival. When I would
drive up he would come out to greet me. When Jesus takes
me home all my loved ones in heaven will come out to greet
me and we'll never be parted again. Those who love God never
part for the last time. In the vocabulary of God there is no such
word as "good-by."

4. *He will keep me at His side forever.* This is the best
part of it all. He tells us that those who trust Him shall reign
forever with Him. We shall be with Him for a thousand years
upon the earth and then through the endless ages in glory.

We won't suffer any pain then, we'll never get sick. We'll
never have any trouble, we'll never grow tired, we'll never die.
No wonder I love Jesus when I think of what He has done,
what He is doing and what He is going to do.

Hyman Appleman, the Jewish evangelist, was converted
in 1925. His family turned upon him and this grieved him
greatly. In 1933 when he was pastor of a church in Texas, his
father came to see him. Day and night during the visit his father
begged him to give up Christ, while the son sought to win

the father to the Saviour. The father refused even to look at a New Testament. He just held out his hands to his son, begging him to give up Christ and come home. When the day of his departure came Hyman sat with his father in the Pullman car and again the father begged him to give up the Saviour. "Mother and I are getting old," he said, "give up Christ and come on home. We have money, we'll care for you."

But Hyman answered, "I can't do it, father. It is impossible." Tears were running down the old man's cheek. Soon the conductor called, "All aboard." Then Hyman leaned over and kissed his father and said, "This is for mother. Tell her that whatever happens I love her." Then he kissed his father again and said, "Daddy, this is for you. But one thing I want you to remember. You don't agree with me, but I am honest and sincere about Christ and I love you with all my heart."

Then Hyman jumped off the train, the tears blinding his eyes. He got in his car, leaned over the steering wheel, wept like a baby and poured out his heart to God for his family. Why didn't he go home? The family needed him; they had made him a good offer. He said that all the while he was talking to his father, above his father's head he could see a cross and on that cross his Saviour dying for him. He said that if Christ was willing to do that for him, he could never give Him up. He would love Him and serve Him forever.

That's the way I feel. He died for me. He loves me. He blesses me and cares for me every day. And some day He is going to do something even more wonderful for me. That's why I love Him. I wish you would fall in love with Him, too.

# 3.

# The Greatest Sentence Ever Written

## I John 4:8b

Many Christians would say that John 3:16 is the greatest sentence ever written: "For God so loved the world, that he gave his only begotten Son, that whosoever believeth in him should not perish, but have everlasting life." Oh, there is no doubt about the greatness of these immortal words. They tell of God's love and Christ's sacrifice for us and of our only hope of salvation. This sentence covers heaven and earth, this life and the life to come. The tiny child learns this verse, the young man lives by it, the middle-aged man leans upon it, the aged man puts all of his hope in it.

There are twenty-five words in John 3:16, but my text, which has only three words in it, is greater than John 3:16. It envelops John 3:16. It includes everything in John 3:16. In fact, John 3:16 is possible because of my text. My text simply says, "God is love." Now if that were not true there would be no John 3:16, no gift of God's Son, no hope for you and me.

When we say that God is love some people say, "I wonder if that is really true." They have been going through the deep waters, pain and suffering have been their lot, their hearts have been broken over some disappointment. They are inclined to say, "If God is love, why did He let all these things happen to me?" But I hope I can show you in this message that God is love in every circumstance of life, through every day, over all the way.

Now what is love? Is it some overpowering physical force which draws two people together? Is it only that? No, it is a thousand times more than that. It is that deep emotion which craves to bless and delights to commune. It is a quenchless desire for the well-being of the beloved. If you really love

29

someone it is more than a mere physical attraction. You delight to be with your beloved, you want sweet fellowship with him, and you want everything good for your beloved, even though it often means the giving of your very self.

And that multiplied ten thousand times over is a picture of God's love. He wants to commune with us, He wants to bless us, He wants the best things for us in time and eternity. And this is the love which made Him give His only Begotten Son for you and me, for in giving Christ He gave Himself.

## I. God Is Love in the Manner of His Giving

Many men of this world have given their wealth, their time, their talents, their very lives to some great cause. But no human being is as generous as God. It is His nature to give, He cannot help it. He loves, therefore He gives.

He loved us by giving us life. All the golden hours and days and years of life are ours because of His love. And then when we misused life and went down into sin, He reached down His loving hand to pull us up and save us. And how did He do it? Was it an easy thing for God to save us? Did He do it by a spoken word, by a twist of the wrist, a nod of the head? No, the hardest thing God ever did was that which He did to save us. He had an only begotten Son whom He loved with all His heart. But He gave Him up to save us poor sinners.

We know that Christ suffered greatly on the cross, but His suffering was no greater than that of the Father. Every lash that cut the back of Christ cut the heart of God. Every thorn that pierced the brow of Christ pierced the heart of God. Every nail driven in the hands and feet of Christ was driven in the heart of God. Every groan that Christ uttered broke the heart of God. Do you see what I mean when I say that God showed His love by giving?

A good woman in New York City had a dear friend in college. After graduation she lost sight of her friend for eighteen long years. Then one day in another city she looked up to a second-story window and saw her old friend. She looked quite old, her hair was gray. The woman on the street went to the door and a maid answered. When she gave her card to the maid, saying, "Take this up to your mistress," the maid answered, "She is not at home." "Yes, she is," the lady said, "I saw her at the window." She pushed past the maid and dashed upstairs. Soon her arms were around her old friend. "Where have you been all these years?" she asked. "Come into the other room and I will show you." She followed her friend into a magnificently furnished room, where she found a seventeen-year old boy who had the mind of a tiny baby.

"My duty is here," said her friend, "here with my darling boy." "How can you stand it?" she asked. And her friend answered, "It is no burden, no care, no trouble to love and serve my boy. And if he ever gives one sign of recognition that I am his mother, I will be well-repaid for all the years of love I have lavished on him."

Now, that's love, human love, a love that gives without stint or hope of reward. And God's love is a billion times greater. He loves, so He must give. It doesn't matter who you are. God loved you and gave His Son for you. This is true of the worst sinner and the greatest saint. If you had been the only person in the world, I tell you that He loved you enough to give His Son for you. He loves the cultured man on the avenue. He loves the savage in darkest Africa. He gave because of that love.

## II. God Is Love in the Manner in Which He Treats Sin

1. *He convicts of sin.* Before Jesus went away He said, "I shall send the Holy Spirit and He shall convict of sin, righteousness and judgment" (John 16:8). And the Holy Spirit does just that. There comes a time in every man's life when the Spirit says to him, "This thing you are doing is wrong. The way you are living is not pleasing in the sight of God." That conviction may come through a sermon, it may come through a song, it may come through a sorrow. But in some way the Holy Spirit points out a person's sin and shows him his need of repentance.

2. *He forgives sin.* Isaiah 55:7 — "Let the wicked forsake his way, and the unrighteous man his thoughts: and let him return unto the Lord, and he will have mercy upon him; and to our God, for he will abundantly pardon."

Christ did not talk much about God's power, but He talked much about His love. And He showed how that love was manifested in the forgiveness of sin. He told of a shepherd who lost one sheep and how he went out into the cold dark night to find it. He told of a father who lost his boy to the far country and how, when the boy returned, he threw his arms around him and welcomed him home. And the shepherd in the story was God. And the father in the story was God. 'Tis God who loves so much that He seeks sinners to forgive and save them.

A mother asked her little boy the question, "If you could say just one thing to God, what would it be?" And the little boy answered, "I would say, 'Oh, God, love me when I am naughty.'" And that's the cry of every heart. That's what God always does.

One boy said to his brother, "We must be good, for if we are not good, father will not love us." Their father overheard this remark and hastened to correct his son, "You are wrong, my son, I love you because you are my son. I love you when you are good and when you are bad. When you are good I love you with a love that makes me glad. When you are bad I love you with a love that makes me sad." And God's love is not conditioned by circumstances. The sun shines on the just and the unjust. It must shine because it is light. So God cannot love some and not love others, because He is love. He loves us when we are what we ought to be, with a love that rejoices. When we have sinned He loves us with a love that forgives.

Now is God's forgiveness automatic? Does God forgive us as we go on in sin? That is the popular conception today. A popular song says, "Although He is grieved by the way we live, He always says, I forgive." But God never promises to forgive our sin unless we repent of it. However, His love is so great that He stands ready to forgive us when we do turn from our sin and turn to Him.

3. *He punishes sin.* Even in this He is showing His love for us. The Bible says, "For whom the Lord loveth he chasteneth, and scourgeth every son whom he receiveth" (Hebrews 12:6). Some fathers are so unwise and so selfish that they will not punish their children, even when it is for the children's good.

It hurts these parents to punish their children, so they let them go and they often go to the devil.

I knew a man whose son was quite ill. The father said, "If he gets well, I will never punish him again." He was doing the worst thing he could do for that boy. If we sinned and God let us continue in sin without punishment, we would become completely evil and rotten. So in love He punishes us. He draws us back into the paths of righteousness by the cords of chastisement and discipline.

A certain man was a good man, but not a Christian. One night when he came home he found his little girl quite ill. In a few days she was dead. The broken-hearted father knelt by the casket and promised God that he would take Christ as his Saviour and Lord. But soon he had forgotten his promise and became enmeshed again in the things of the world. Sometime later his other daughter died. This time he knelt down again and made God the same promise. But this time he kept his promise. Years later a preacher was visiting in his home. The man said to the preacher, "Come and take a ride with me." They rode out to the cemetery and the man told the preacher his story as he stood between the two little graves. Then they knelt down and the preacher prayed. As they left the cemetery, the man said to the preacher, "Doctor, I pity a man whom God hasn't chastened."

A wise father doesn't chastise a child because he is stronger than the child or because he dislikes the child. He chastises the child because he loves that child and wants that child to grow into the finest man or woman. And God the Father chastises us because He loves us and wants us to grow into the likeness of His dear Son.

### III. God Is Love in the Time of Trouble

Israel was almost drowned in trouble because of her sinfulness and idolatry, but we read in Isaiah 63:9 that "in all their affliction he was afflicted." Isaiah was simply saying that God suffered when they suffered. It is true today, also. God knows our sorrows and sympathizes with us. He says: "As one whom his mother comforteth, so will I comfort you" (Isaiah 66:13).

Oh, how sweet is the comfort of a loving mother. You may become separated from your mother by the river of death, but there is One who is the same yesterday, today and forever, and the mother heart of God is never turned away from us.

In the years of my ministry I have known many people who suffered from trouble and heartbreak. Some could see no reason in it at all, they could not understand why these things happened to them, so they rebelled against God. But I have known others who could look through their tears and see the face of God and who knew that all was well. Yes, even when we go through the deep waters we can say, "God is still love. I know that He loves me and will not send me more than He and I can bear together."

### IV. God Is Love When We Come to the End of the Way

The realization that God is love robs death of its sting and its power to frighten. Because God loves we know that some day He is going to give us something better than this world. He is going to lift us out of all our pain and trouble and tears and take us to a house not made with hands, where Jesus awaits us and where joys immortal flow.

What is death for the child of God? It is the sleep that the Father gives to His beloved. It is the kindly nurse who puts us to bed. It is the rest that God gives to His tired child. It is laying aside every earthly care and burden and finding peace. It is giving up the cross and receiving the crown.

Yes, God is love all the way from grace to glory. His love for us began before we were born and will last throughout eternity. How tragically lost and undone we would be without the love of God. And we can never be separated from that love.

Romans 8:35-39 — "Who shall separate us from the love of Christ? shall tribulation, or distress, or persecution, or famine, or nakedness, or peril, or sword? As it is written, For thy sake we are killed all the day long; we are accounted as sheep for the slaughter. Nay, in all these things we are more than conquerors through him that loved us. For I am persuaded that neither death, nor life, nor angels, nor principalities, nor powers, nor things present, nor things to come, Nor height, nor death, nor any other creature, shall be able to separate us from the love of God, which is in Christ Jesus our Lord."

Now in view of God's great love for us, we ought to love Him the more. We ought to put our lives in His hands. We'll never be worth anything unless we do.

An Oriental legend tells us of a king who sat upon his royal throne on a certain day while his people brought their gifts to show him how much they loved him. Great and wealthy men brought their jewels and gold and silver and laid them at his feet. Finally a poor woman came. She had only a penny. She said to herself, "I can't give that to him." Then she thought a minute and said, "Yes, I'll do it. He will understand."

So she went forward and dropped the penny in his hand and turned away, ashamed. But the king called her back. He opened his hand and, behold, the penny had turned into a gold coin. "Did you give me this gold coin?" he asked the woman. She replied, "No, I have not seen one of these in a long time." But the king said, "Yes, but you put it in my hand and I have held it ever since." "No, sire," she said, "I have never seen it." Then the king said, "Take it back into your hand." She did so and the gold coin became a penny again. She put it back in the king's hand and it became a gold coin again.

It is the same way with our lives. If we keep them for ourselves, if we spend them for this world, they are worth nothing. But if we put them in God's hands, they will be transformed and made beautiful and useful. What are you going to do with your life? Are you going to keep it for yourself or use it for this God of love?

# 4.

# Crumbling Foundations
# in American Life

Matthew 7:24-29

If anything on this earth is going to last it must have a good foundation. When they erect a building in New York that is a hundred stories high, they first go down deep into the rock to secure a firm foundation. Then the winds and storms may beat upon that building, and it will still stand. Organizations must have a firm foundation. They must be built on the foundation of a great purpose, high principles and staunch personnel. Nations must have a firm foundation. Babylon was founded upon lust and wealth and it fell. Rome was founded upon pleasure and power and it fell.

America was founded upon a firm foundation. You remember the story of Roger Babson and the South American president. The president said to Mr. Babson, "Why is it that North America is so far ahead of South America in so many ways? We have great natural resources, a fine climate and many other things conducive to growth and success. Why is North America so far ahead of us?" Mr. Babson then said, "Why do you think this is so?" And the president said, "I believe it is because South America was settled by men who were looking for gold, and North America was settled by men who were looking for God." Yes, America was founded upon a firm foundation, and she will continue as long as we build upon that foundation.

In our text Jesus tells the story of two houses. One of them was built upon the sand and the other was built upon the rock. The same storm hit both of these houses. One of them fell and the other stood. Why? Because one of them was built

37

upon a solid foundation and the other was not. I want to talk to you today about four things upon which our great country was founded. Then I think that you can easily see that these foundations are crumbling.

## I. The Old-Fashioned Christian Home

Robert Burns, one of Scotland's great poets, wrote *The Cotter's Saturday Night.* In this poem he pictures the home-coming on Saturday night of a simple laboring man. This man is warmly greeted by his wife and children. We can see them as they move into the house. The man has his arms around those whom he loves and all of them are very happy as they are together again. That night they eat their frugal meal, after giving thanks to God for it. After the dishes have been done and the chores completed they gather around the old organ and sing the songs of Zion. When the bedtime hour comes, the father takes down the heavy family Bible. He runs his fingers over the words in the great Book and haltingly reads to his family of the things of God. Then he falls upon his knees and prays God's blessings upon his humble home. The poet then says, "From scenes like these old Scotia's grandeur springs, which makes her loved at home and revered abroad." No wonder Scotland became the cradle of real religion. It was founded upon a rock.

Our early American homes were old-fashioned Christian homes. The days were spent in work and the nights were spent at home. The men had their place and the women had theirs. The fireside was the throne, the father was the king, the mother the queen and the children the subjects. They had time for the Bible, time for prayer and time for the church. These homes made our country what it is.

Today our homes are different. The world calls and we answer. We have too little time for our homes. Night comes on and we don't know where the children are. Often the children don't know where the parents are. The Bible is forgotten, prayer is left out, the church is ignored. The majority of our homes are not Christian homes any more. Let us look at some of the causes of this decline.

1. *Too many outside activities.* We read daily of our people going to this party and the other one, to this club and the other one. They have no time left for the home. We may suppose that there is no harm in these activities, yet there is often this resulting harm — our children and our homes are neglected. Oh, may God give us people who prefer the favor of the Lord rather than the favor of the world, who had rather have it written in heaven that they are faithful than to get their names in the social column.

2. *Too many outside organizations.* We read often of the activities of certain people. They have a long list of organizations behind their names. We know then that they are neglecting their homes, their church and their children. I have learned this, namely, that if you keep faithful to your church you will have little time for outside worldly organizations. At the same time you will be doing a thousand times more good in the world.

Some years ago a woman who was a member of the church where I was pastor said to me, "I am sorry I cannot come to church, but my boy is sick and I have to look after him." At that time I was asked to come out for several nights and help in the rehearsal of a charity play. We stayed there many nights until midnight and that woman was there every night. She had her boy with her also. Why can't Christians be consistent?

3. *Too many outside attractions.* I am not saying that you should never go to some of the things that are clean and wholesome, but some people run this matter into the ground. They feel that they must go to everything that comes to town. They have lost the meaning of "home, sweet home."

4. *Too little parental discipline.* In former days the word of the parents was law. Father and mother were looked up to by the children. But today the children resent parental control. The Bible says, "Children obey your parents" (Ephesians 6:1). Today the children say, "Parents, you must do as we say." The Bible says, "Train up a child in the way he should go" (Proverbs 22:6). Today the children say, "Let's bring our parents up-to-date." God tells us to honor our fathers and mothers. He adds the promise of long life to that commandment. Oh, that our

homes were ideal Christian homes! If there ever was a time when our parents need to pray, it is now. They need all the help that they can get.

The great evangelist, J. Wilbur Chapman, was walking down the street with a friend in the city of Washington. This friend pointed to the glistening dome of the capitol and said, "There is the heart of our nation." But Mr. Chapman replied, "You are wrong. The heart of our nation is in her homes." As goes the home so goes the nation. If our homes fail, all that is good in our country will be lost. But this is one of the foundations which is crumbling.

### II. The Second Foundation Is the Proper Observance of the Lord's Day

God created the world and rested upon the seventh day. He said, "Remember the Sabbath day, to keep it holy" (Exodus 20:8). That was the Jewish Sabbath and it was kept until the Resurrection of Christ. Then God did something more wonderful than creating a world. He completed redemption for all mankind. That redemption was completed when the crucified Saviour became the risen Redeemer. Today we call this day the Lord's Day. We are to observe it in His honor.

In the olden days Sunday was set aside for church and worship, and rest. Today it is used much for recreation, sports and a good time. Some people say that the times have changed. Yes, they have changed, but God has not changed and His laws have not been changed. There is more than one way to desecrate the Sabbath. You can get in your car and ride all over the country and that is desecration. You can turn your back upon your church and visit all of your relatives on Sunday. That is a desecration. You can work in your yard on Sunday, as many people do, and that is desecration. You can stay at home and read the papers or you can go fishing. All of this is a desecration of the Lord's Day. In fact, anything that keeps you from God's house can be classified as desecration, unless it is something providential like sickness or some similar cause.

A man stood by the window in the home of his friend and looked out toward the river. The friend said to him, "Beyond that river there is a small town, but you can see it only on Sunday." "Why only on Sunday?" asked the man. His friend replied, "On the other days the smoke of the factories settles down about the town and hides it. The factories are closed on Sunday and then you can see the town." Yes, the dust of the world gets in our eyes, but on the Lord's Day that dust ought to be settled. Then we can see God and the pathway leading to heaven.

Some people say, "I work hard all the week and I must rest on Sunday." Who gave you the strength to do this work? It was God Himself. Don't you think that He ought to be recognized? A consecrated Christian says, "I have a hard week coming up. I need the strength and the help that comes from a Sunday spent in God's house."

But this is one of the crumbling foundations in American life — God's Holy Day has become man's holiday.

### III. Another Foundation That Is Crumbling Is Belief in God's Word

In the olden days men said, "This is God's Word and I dare not go against it." Today the Bible is thrown aside and men go out and do as they please. We have even come to the time when some preachers say, "You can't believe all of the Bible." Some of the professors in our schools are saying that they are exercising academic freedom when they teach that the Bible is full of myths and contradictions. Now the Bible tells us about the sinfulness of man, his accountability to God and punishment for sin. Of course, this doesn't please the natural man. So he closes his eyes to Bible truth, throws away all moral restraint and goes the limit.

You say that you believe the Bible and then live as if you had never heard of it. You never check your life by it. You ought to examine your life and see if you are living up to the teachings of the Word of God. The Bible will tell you how to live. It says, "Seek ye first the kingdom of God, and his righteousness" (Matthew 6:33). Are you doing that? It says, "Abstain from all appearance of evil" (I Thessalonians 5:22). Are you doing that? It says, "Bring ye all the tithes into the storehouse" (Malachi 3:10). Are you doing that? It says, "Pray without ceasing" (I Thessalonians 5:17). Are you doing that? It says, "Be kind one to another . . . forgive one another" (Ephesians 4:32). Are you doing that? How does your life measure up with the teachings of the Bible?

Every good thing in our national life is based upon the Bible. Our laws, our hospitals, our childrens' homes and every humanitarian institution that we have sprang from the Bible. If we let the foundations crumble our nation is in great danger. We are to learn the Bible, we are to love the Bible, we are to live the Bible.

### IV. Another Foundation That Is Crumbling Is Love for Christ's Church

You have seen the picture of the Pilgrims trudging through the snow on their way to the church. The father in the family had a gun over his shoulder and a Bible in his hand. He was leading his whole family to church. They knew then that they needed what the church could give them. How much more do we need it today! God has put the church down here to help men, to point them to heaven. But many people criticize the church. They never darken its doors, they never give it a thought until sickness or death come. But if all the churches and their influence were taken out of America, it would not be a fit place in which to live. We might as well change its name to hell.

It's an amazing thing to see men who are so faithful to their wives and their home on Sunday, but they can't come to church. Yet every other day in the week is spent in some worldly pursuit. Just let it rain a few drops and they say that they can't go to church. Yet you will find them at their place of business on Monday. Two men were out fishing one Sunday and when eleven o'clock came one of them said, "We ought not to be out here fishing, we ought to be in church listening to our pastor." And the other one replied, "I couldn't go to church if I were at home. My wife is sick."

Why do men neglect the church? It is because their hearts are not right with God. They are lacking in love for the One who has done more for them than anyone else. Jesus loved the church and gave Himself for it. If you love it you will give it your best. You will never lift your hand nor your voice against it. In the Book of Revelation we see Christ standing in the midst of the churches. He is still there. If you try to hurt or break up the fellowship of the church you will have to account to Him for it.

We need the church, not just as a place to which to go, but as a force to help us to live and help us to die. Let us come to it for that help in these trying days. Let us bring it our best. Let us bring it our time, our talents, our tithe and our service.

These are the four foundations of our good way of life — the Christian home, the Christian Sabbath, the Christian Book and the Christian church. They are divine things and we must forever hold them dear.

## V. Look at the Results of This Neglect

1. *There has been a lowering of our entire national life.* We have crooked politics and crooked politicians. We have graft and betrayal of trusts. We have divorces and juvenile delinquency. We have vandalism and hoodlumism. Our young people are caught in the toils of sin and crime. We have every other evil of society and all of it comes out of the breakdown of these four divine things. God has said that righteousness exalteth a nation" (Proverbs 14:34). A nation is made of people. If you and I live the wrong lives the nation will be wrong. If you and I are right in our living we will help hold the country close to God's throne.

The old railroad ran from Cripple Creek to Colorado Springs. It was forty miles long and it had a drop of four thousand feet in this distance. Derailing switches were all along the way. If a single car got loose and started down the tracks it might destroy a whole train of cars. So when this happened the trainman would wire ahead and a switchman would throw the derailing switch and the car would be thrown off the track. The history of the world is filled with derailing switches. When nations forget God, He derails them into oblivion. America will stand as long as she holds on to God.

2. *Another result of this neglect is broken homes.* God has ordained that happiness should reign in our homes. But when sin comes in and God is left out the home is broken to pieces. If our homes are centered in Christ, and the church has its rightful place, we will not have the problem of broken homes.

3. *Another result of this neglect is blasted character.* Character is blasted and broken when God is forgotten. Men try the things of this world and become disappointed with them. They fail to try the things which make for character.

4. *Another result of this neglect is the broken hearts of parents.* Parents can go on now, paying no attention to the preacher or to the church or to God. But some day their children will be living in sin and they will leave them sitting in sorrow. In some homes the parents make it a habit to criticize the preacher and the church and those who represent God. By so doing they are tearing down something in the lives of their children. They will weep over this some day. After I had preached one day on comfort in the time of sorrow, a woman said to me, "A living sorrow is worse than a dead one." That is certainly true. Your neglect of the things of God may bring you a broken heart.

## VI. God Has the Remedy for the Situation

God says, "If my people, which are called by my name, shall humble themselves, and pray, and seek my face, and turn from their wicked ways; then will I hear from heaven, and will forgive their sin, and will heal their land" (II Chronicles 7:14). He also said, "Return unto me and I will return unto you."

1. *This means a return to God in the home.* It means trying to set up a Christian home where love and prayer permeate everything. I would like to ask you mothers and fathers to do one thing. Go tonight into the room where your children are sleeping. Look down upon them and think of what you owe them. Then get down upon your knees and ask God to help you to be a better father or a better mother.

2. *This means a return to God in the proper observance of the Lord's Day.* Develop some convictions along these lines. Use the day for rest and worship and service.

3. *This means a return to God and love for the Bible.* Go home and dust off your Bible. Read it and begin to live by it.

4. *This means a return to God in love for His church.* Resolve to attend the church faithfully. You will find there the greatest help in the world. Resolve to give it your best. It's a great privilege to have a part in His work. Resolve to serve in your church and that will bring you the greatest joy. Then when He comes He will find you faithful.

Let me tell you the story of Greyfriar's Bobby. In Edinburgh, Scotland, there is a famous water fountain. There is a statue of a dog on the top of this fountain, a dog named Bobby. Bobby was a shepherd's dog. One day the dog followed the old shepherd to town and that day the shepherd dropped dead upon the street. The undertaker took the body to a funeral parlor and the dog followed. They had to kick him out when they closed the place that night. The next day Bobby followed the funeral procession to the Greyfriar's churchyard where the old shepherd was buried. He stayed by the grave until everyone had left. He lay down near the head of the grave and the sexton tried to entice him away, but the dog would not move. So the sexton each day brought food and water to the faithful dog. One night a deep snow came and the next morning when the sexton went out to look for Bobby he found only a mound of snow on the grave. Bobby was beneath the snow. He had stayed by his master until he had frozen to death. He had been faithful unto death.

Oh, if a dog can be faithful to his master like that, how much more faithful should we be. We have a greater Master, the Lord Jesus Christ. Let's be faithful to Him and then all the foundations will be secure.

# 5.

# The Sun Is Shining and I Am Blind

## II Corinthians 4:3-6

Some time ago, in one of our southern cities, I saw a blind beggar sitting on a little stool and leaning up against the building. When I went up close to him to put a coin in his cup, I saw a sign around his neck with these words on it: "THE SUN IS SHINING AND I AM BLIND." This message struck me with great pathos. Here was a man who realized that he was in a world of beauty, but he couldn't see it and he couldn't enjoy it because he was blind. Then I thought of the thousands of people in this world who are in far worse condition. They are spiritually blind. The sun of God's love and goodness and grace and salvation is shining, but they are blind to it all.

The Bible speaks of many blind people. Jesus met scores of them as He traveled the roads of Palestine. He was always touched by their plight and He always stopped and gave them their sight. In like manner over the years He has opened up the eyes of countless thousands so that they might see the glory of God in salvation. Oh, that tonight He might open other eyes, eyes that have been blinded by sin.

The text speaks of "the god of this world." Who is he? It is Satan. He is the one that men are following today. He is the one who is blinding the eyes of men. He doesn't want the light of the Gospel to shine in their hearts. He doesn't want them to be saved. Therefore, he blinds men to the most glorious things of heaven and earth. What does a man like Khrushchev know about the goodness of God? What does he know about the atoning blood of Christ? What does he know about the work of the Holy Spirit, or regeneration, or justification, or the joys of the Christian life? He knows nothing. His eyes have been blinded by Satan. I have used Khrushchev simply as an

47

example. The same is true of every unsaved man. The sinner is a foreigner to all of these things.

## I. The Devil Blinds Men to the Goodness of God

Anyone on this earth who doesn't realize that God has been good to him is certainly blind. Jeremiah said, "Thy mercies are new every morning" (Lamentations 3:22, 23). How true that is. Every morning when we wake up we are simply surrounded by the goodness and love of a great God. We ought to begin the day by thanking God for all of His goodness. During the depression I visited a man and talked to him about his relationship to God. He lived in a nice home in the best part of the city. He had been a plant superintendent, but because of business conditions the plant had to be shut down. He was given a smaller job at less salary. But he did have a job while others lost their jobs. He began to complain to me about his bad fortune. Then I looked around at the nicely furnished house and said, "But, after all, God has been good to you." And he replied, "I don't know so much about that." He had no appreciation for the things he enjoyed. He was blind to the goodness of God.

The song says, "Count your Blessings." This is a good exercise. Instead of looking at your troubles, look at your blessings. Instead of looking down, look up to God. If a man can look around him today and not find much to be thankful for, he is blind indeed. We live in a great country while many others live in practical slavery. We have perfect freedom, while others do not enjoy this freedom. We have religious liberty while many are denied this liberty. We have an abundance of things to eat, good clothes to wear, cars, television, and a thousand other things which other people do not have.

Who are we to complain when we think about the goodness of God? And of course, He reached the heights of love and goodness when He gave His Son to die for us.

## II. The Devil Blinds Men to Their Own Spiritual Condition

It doesn't matter how a man looks to other men, but it matters greatly how he looks to God. In the eyes of the world a man may be very wonderful and fine, but in the eyes of God he is just another poor sinner.

Clark Gable was a great movie actor. He was handsome and suave and talented. Out in Hollywood they called him "the king." Men admired him and women fell in love with him. He was married several times, he lived in fine homes, he made a fortune. I believe that he won two Oscars for being the best actor of the year. He died a few years ago. I wonder how he appeared in God's sight. I know that all of his fame and popularity didn't count with God. I wonder if his soul had been washed in the blood of the Lamb. I am just saying to you what the Bible says, "Man looks upon the outward appearance, but God looks upon the heart" (I Samuel 16:7).

What is the condition of a lost man before God? The Bible says that he is a sinner. The Bible says that he is condemned. The Bible says that he is dead. The Bible says that the wrath of God abideth on him. The Bible says that hell is waiting for him. The Bible says that he will be turned into hell. The Bible says that he will be cast into the lake of fire. On the other hand, what does the Bible say about the man who does come to Christ? It tells us that his sins will be forgiven. It tells us that there will be no condemnation for him. It tells us that he will have the friendship of God. It tells us that he will live forever in eternal glory.

Of course, the devil will try to pull the wool over your eyes. He will tell you how good you are. He will tell you that God loves you so much that He won't let you go to hell. He will tell you that everyone is a child of God and that everyone is going to heaven. All this is the devil's lie. Don't let him fool you. Salvation is in Christ alone. Open up your eyes, see yourself as God sees you, then do something about it.

### III. The Devil Blinds Men as to Bible Truth

You tried to read your Bible and you came to a part which was not too interesting and which you did not understand. Then the devil said to you, "The Bible is too hard to understand. Forget it." And you did. Now the Bible tells us that spiritual things must be spiritually discerned. You can't understand the

Bible until the Spirit of God lives within you. This comes when you surrender to Christ.

The devil says, "Sure, buy yourself a good Bible. Put it on the table. Carry it under your arm when you come to Sunday school. But don't read it and don't fashion your life according to its teachings." Yes, the devil will blind your mind as to Bible truth.

### IV. The Devil Blinds Men as to the Way of Salvation

In the early years of my ministry I heard preachers say, "Men think that they can be saved by their good works, their good deeds, their fine lives." And I said, "No, everyone knows that you are not saved by what you do or by what you are, but by repentance and faith." But I know now that these preachers were right. The average man apart from Christ today will tell you all the good things you can do to be saved. But Christ has no part in his plan of salvation.

There is only one way of salvation. It is not through a church, nor through a man, nor through a form, nor through a good deed. Do you want to be saved? The Bible is our only guidebook in the matter of salvation. It tells us that we must repent of our sins and put our faith in Jesus Christ. This is not just a matter of mental assent. It includes a whole change of heart and life. It means a right-about-face. It means simply leaning on the strong arm of Jesus.

> In my hand no price I bring,
> Simply to Thy cross I cling.

Up in Chicago some years ago there was a nightclub called, "The Gates of Hell." This club was just a few doors down the street from Calvary Church. One night a drunk man stopped a young fellow on the street and asked him to show him the way to "The Gates of Hell." The young man pointed to a sign on the corner which read "Calvary Church" and said to him, "Just go right by Calvary and you will come to 'The Gates of Hell.'" How true that is! The cross of Jesus Christ stands between you and hell. If you go by that cross, if you trample Jesus under foot, you will land in hell.

Yes, one of the devil's big lies today is to tell you that there is some other way of salvation, but,

> I must needs go home by the way of the cross,
> There's no other way but this.
> I shall ne'er catch sight of the gates of light,
> If the way of the cross I miss.

## V. The Devil Blinds Men to the Joys of the Christian Life

Do you know what the devil tells people? He says, "Look at those Christians. They don't have any fun. They can't do half of the things that you do. Their lives are bound up by a set of rules found in the Bible and they are miserable." Oh, what a lie that is! Christians have a peace and a joy in their hearts which the world can neither give nor take away. Line up one hundred real Christians on one side of this room and line up a hundred worldlings on the other side. I guarantee that you will find much more happiness in the lives of the Christians than you will find in this other group.

A certain man lived in the slums of a great city. Every day he looked upon the poverty around him. The plaster was crumbling, the curtains were frayed, the divan had collapsed and the floors were bare. As he looked out of his window, he saw only dingy walls, ragged children, forlorn women and hollow-eyed men. But often in his despondency he closed his eyes and dreamed. He saw himself in a beautiful home, with fine rugs on the floor, pictures on the wall and beautiful furniture in every room. The home was surrounded by trees and flowers. He had everything that his heart could desire. But it was only a dream. Then one day he received an official letter. The letter told him that a long-forgotten relative had died and had left him a great estate and a huge fortune. He couldn't believe it. He hadn't seen that relative in years. He thought someone was playing a practical joke on him. So he threw the letter in the fire and continued to chafe in poverty and the slums.

There are many men like that today. They would like to have happiness of heart and peace of mind. They would like to go to heaven at the end of the way. But they let the devil tell them that there are no joys in the Christian life and they live on in shallows and in misery.

### VI. The Devil Blinds Men as to the Certainty of Death and Judgment

The Bible tells us that "it is appointed unto men once to die, but after this the judgment" (Hebrews 9:27). All men know that. They know that this life isn't all. They know that they must die and face the judgment. But the devil makes them forget all about it and they do nothing about their relationship to God.

Rev. Jack Hyles, pastor of the First Baptist Church of Hammond, Indiana, formerly served in Texas. His father was a drinking man, and was separated from his family. On the last day in 1949 Jack found his father in a saloon. He had never been in a saloon before, but he walked up to the bar and said to his father, "Dad, you are going home with me tonight. Tomorrow is New Year's Day and you are going to hear me preach." His father said, "I am not going." "Dad," said the preacher, "you are bigger than I am, but if you don't come with me, I am going to make a scene and embarrass you." Finally the father went home with the son. Jack took him to the watch night party on Saturday night. During the party he said to his father, "Dad, are you having a good time?" "Yes, son," he said, "they don't have good times like this where I go." Then the son said, "Dad, I want you to be saved and be one of my deacons some day." The old man said, "Son, I would like to be one of your deacons." The son urged the father to receive Christ but he refused. On Sunday the father sat in the church while the son preached. He begged the lost to come to Christ, but he was talking mostly to his father. One of the deacons who sat near his father put his arm around him and urged him to go forward, but the old man would not make a move. That afternoon Jack said, "Dad, I am a preacher. You drink and curse and our home is broken. Won't you receive Christ as your Saviour and live a good life?" The tears came into the old man's eyes and he said, "Son, I am going to do it, but not now. I am going back to Dallas and this spring I will come back here and open up a little store. I will accept Christ and let you baptize me." That was all that the preacher could get his father to say. That was on January 1, 1950. Jack said that every time he baptized anyone he pictured himself baptizing his big daddy. On May 13th his phone rang with a long distance call. A man on the other end of the wire said, "This is Mr. Smith. Your dad dropped dead on the job today." The heart of the young preacher broke as he followed the hearse to the cemetery a day or two later. He felt that his father was not ready to meet God.

Oh, that is the trouble with men today. They know what they ought to do, but they think they have plenty of time. Who knows when you will hear another sermon? Who knows when you will have another opportunity to accept Christ? Before sunrise you or I may be called upon to meet God.

## VII. Finally the Devil Blinds Men as to the Happiness of Heaven

As no human tongue can tell of the agonies of hell, neither can anyone describe all the glories of heaven. The devil blinds men to the joys of it. But if we could only know all the wonderful things awaiting us out there, nothing could prevent our getting ready for it.

The best friend I ever had was Forrest C. Garrard of Atlanta, Georgia. He was the finest and sweetest Christian I ever knew. He had more of the Spirit of Christ than any man I ever met. He was an executive with the Chevrolet Company. He had a big job and a good salary. But he gave all of this up and became the pastor of a country church. He had me to come and help him in six revivals. Oh, how he loved people! And how he loved the Lord, and how hard he worked for the Saviour. Then on Sunday night before Christmas, 1958, he was on his way to church. He said to his wife, "I don't feel so good." He pulled the car over to the side of the road, fell over the steering wheel and was gone in a minute.

Now I know that he is enjoying the happiness of heaven. His picture is on the wall in my office. I look at that picture and long to see him again. And some day, by the grace of God, I hope to go out and join my Saviour and see this dear friend and all my loved ones in a land where we never grow old.

"The Sun Is Shining and I am Blind." The sun of God's grace and love and salvation is shining for you tonight. Don't let the devil blind you to all that the Lord can do for you.

# 6.

# Because of Calvary

Matthew 27:33-36

On the darkest day that ever dawned Jesus Christ was crucified. Just the night before He had dined with His friends. He knew what was to come upon Him and He told them about it. But one of them denied Him with an oath and another betrayed Him for thirty pieces of silver. He had been arrested, He had been dragged from one court to another, He had been beaten and spat upon and humiliated. Although He was God's Son from heaven, the foul hands of wicked men were laid on Him.

There had been no sleep for Him that night. And in the early dawn they took Him out to Calvary's hill. They nailed Him to a Roman cross and lifted Him up between heaven and earth, there to die in excruciating pain. There He hangs, nailed there by our sins. There He hangs, dying in our stead. There He hangs, loving us in spite of our sins. There He hangs, dying that we might forever live.

Yes, that was the darkest day in the world's history. But because of that day the whole world is brighter. Because of that day the whole world knows the love of God which passeth understanding. Because of that day hope is born for every man. And the very minute you and I trust Him as our Saviour, all that He did on the cross is put over to our account. Ah, yes, because of Calvary all good things are ours for time and eternity.

## I. Because of Calvary We Know the Love of God That Passeth All Understanding

Does God love us, we who have sinned against Him? We certainly don't deserve His love. Yet, He shows us His love in a million ways. He shows it by giving us health and strength, by providing our daily bread, by blessing us every minute that we live. When we awake each morning, God gives us a new day because He loves us. The clothes we put on are ours because He loves us. The meals we eat are ours because He loves us. The smiles of our loved ones are ours because He loves us. Our jobs are ours because He loves us.

I remember a dear old colored woman from my boyhood days. She went about our little town, carrying a cloth bag. She delved into the garbage cans and rubbish heaps and when she found anything she thought she could use, she placed it in her bag, saying, "Thank God for that." If we thanked God for everything that came our way, life would be one continual round of thanksgiving.

But God showed His love best when He gave His only begotten Son for our redemption. I wonder if there was any hesitation about this matter on God's part. He looked at us sinners and knew that there was nothing good in us. He knew that we were not worthy of His notice. He knew that we had broken His laws and rebelled against Him. We didn't look very good in His sight. Then He looked at His Son. He was the dearest thing in heaven to God. He was the One altogether lovely. There was no spot or blemish in Him. He was always God's sweet, obedient, loving Son. God's heart must have broken as He made the choice. But we read that, "God so loved the world that he gave his only begotten Son."

And when we see Jesus hanging yonder on the cross, we can hear God saying, "I loved you, didn't I? In spite of all your sin I loved you. Here is proof of that love. I gave My beloved Son for you." Yes, because of Calvary we know how much God loves us.

II. Because of Calvary We Have a Great Saviour
and a Divine Companion

We know anyone can be saved who comes to Christ. He saves unto the uttermost. No one who ever called upon Him for salvation has ever been turned down.

But He not only saves us, He continues with us as a divine

Companion. I read about a man who was drowning. Another man leaped into the water and rescued him. But when the people looked around later for the man's rescuer, he was gone. It is not that way with Christ. He saves us but He never leaves us. He walks by our side every day, guiding, blessing, comforting.

I am thinking now of something that happened several years ago in the Ford Chapel of the First Baptist Church of El Paso. Several years prior to that time Billy Graves had been our Educational Director. But he felt that he ought to go to the seminary and prepare himself for mission work in South America. We reluctantly told him good-by and he and his wife and little daughter left for Fort Worth. We visited them several times while they were in school and had sweet fellowship with them. When they graduated Billy and Ada were appointed as missionaries to Argentina. He could have served as Educational Director in any great church in America, but he felt God's call to Argentina.

Things went well with them in Argentina and they were doing a great work for the Lord. Then Ada became ill and was brought back to Dallas for treatment. Her condition improved and they came out to El Paso where she gave a glowing testimony in our church on Wednesday night. Then she was forced to return to the hospital in Dallas and soon we received news that she had died. Her body was brought back to El Paso and the funeral was held in our chapel. When I came to the pulpit I saw Billy and his daughter, Sally Kate, on the very front row. The chapel was filled with their friends. At Billy's request the congregation sang "Blessed Assurance." I had never heard that hymn used as a congregational song at a funeral.

As the congregation sang I looked at Billy and Sally Kate. The light of heaven was on their faces and they were singing with all the fervor of their souls.

> Blessed assurance, Jesus is mine!
> Oh, what a foretaste of glory divine!

Then I said to myself, "That's what Christ can mean to a Christian. He not only saved these people, He is a living reality in their lives. He walks with them and talks with them every day."

Yes, because of Calvary we have a Saviour who saves us from sin and a divine Companion to walk by our side through the journeys of life.

### III. BECAUSE OF CALVARY WE HAVE A GOSPEL TO PREACH

What does the word "Gospel" mean? It means good news, the news of salvation and hope for a lost world. If a man is ill and the doctor says, "You can go home from the hospital tomorrow and in a few days you'll be well," isn't that good news? If a man is deeply in debt and he learns that he has become the heir to a million dollars, isn't that good news? If you hear that a loved one has been lost at sea and word comes that he is safe, isn't that good news? Yes, but the best news of all is the news that Christ died to give men hope and eternal life. Billy Graham went to Africa and preached to many people who had never heard the Gospel. He said that their faces lighted up when they came to know that God had given His Son to save them from their sins.

This is the message that the world needs to hear today. Every day we hear about crime, we hear about the arms race, we hear about men in outer space, we hear of wars and rumors of war. We need to hear about something else, we need to hear about Jesus. When Dr. Ramsey Pollard preached in Japan, the people said, "All he talks about is Jesus." And that's what preachers ought to talk about. We can get everything else from the newspapers, when we come to church we come to hear about Jesus.

But the preacher is not the only one to carry this gospel message. The layman has valuable contacts which the preacher never has. It is up to you to speak a good word for Jesus. Your friends and fellow-workers are battling against life. Do you ever say, "I know Someone who can help you"?

A young Scottish preacher was preparing to preach his first sermon. He had just received his seminary degree and had accepted his first pastorate. So he summoned all of his book learning and wrote out a learned discourse. His mother lived with him so he took the manuscript in and read it to her. She knew that he was going to preach to very simple people, so she said, "Laddie, when you go to the pulpit, speak a good word for Jesus." He went back to his study and thought about what she had said. He knew his sermon was not right, so he tore up the manuscript and prepared a sermon with Christ as the center. When he preached the next day the blessings of God fell upon his congregation. He had said a good word for Jesus.

Yes, because of Calvary we have a story to tell, a story of love and redeeming grace.

## IV. Because of Calvary We Have a Home Waiting for Us at the End of the Way

Nearly everyone in the world believes in a life after death and a land where we can live forever in eternal joy. And everyone wants to go to that land. But men have different ideas as to how to get there. Some say that we get there because of our good works. They say, "Do good and God will open the gates." Some say that we get there through religious forms and ceremonies. They say that baptism or something else opens the gates of glory. Some say we get there through penance and self-inflicted suffering.

There are many theories about salvation, but only one true way to heaven. The Bible tells us the way. Jesus said, "I am the way, the truth and the life: no man cometh unto the Father, but by me" (John 14:6). Acts 4:12 says, "Neither is there salvation in any other: for there is none other name under heaven given among men, whereby we must be saved." John 1:12 says, "As many as received him, to them gave he power to become the sons of God, even to them that believe on his name."

There are many good things that we can do to obtain salvation, but they all fall short. It is like a man building a ladder on which he can climb to the moon. The climb is all right for a few feet, but the ladder doesn't reach high enough. In order to get to heaven, there is only one ladder — repentance toward God and faith toward the Lord Jesus Christ.

I want you to look at several things that can never happen to us in heaven, all because of Calvary.

1. *We will never suffer the agony of separation.* But Jesus did. After all the ages of sweet fellowship with God, He was separated from Him on the cross. He cried, "My God, my God, why hast thou forsaken Me?" (Matthew 27:46). Why did He utter such a cry? Because He was bearing our sins in His own body on the tree and since God's pure eyes cannot look upon sin, He turned His back upon His Son.

Now the lost sinner will suffer separation from God. Christ can help him now, but after death no prayers of his will be answered, no request that he makes will be granted. In Luke 16 we are told that there is a great gulf between heaven and earth. God never reaches His hand across that gulf to help the sinner. He will help him now if he calls upon Him, but not then.

Can you imagine how it would be to be separated from God here and now? Why, if God took His hands off of us for one minute, we couldn't draw a breath. Oh, the terror, the tragedy of eternal separation from God. But a Christian will never experience separation from God, all because of Calvary.

2. *We will never suffer the agony of shame.* But Jesus did. He was altogether holy, but they stripped Him of His garments and they hung Him naked before the gaze of those around the cross. The child of God will never suffer such shame. Christ was naked, but He has clothed us with His righteousness. He was put to shame that we might be assured of glory. He took the sins of the world upon Himself, that our sins might be forever put away.

The sinner faces nothing but shame when he comes to the end of the way. He finally realizes the enormity of his sin against God, his rejection of Christ. The children of God have not shame, but glory awaiting them.

Listen to Revelation 7:13-17 —"And one of the elders answered, saying unto me, What are these which are arrayed in white robes? and whence came they? And I said unto him, Sir, thou knowest. And he said to me, These are they which came out of great tribulation, and have washed their robes, and made them white in the blood of the Lamb. Therefore are they before the throne of God, and serve him day and night in his temple: and he that sitteth on the throne shall dwell among them. They shall hunger no more, neither thirst any more; neither shall the sun light on them, nor any heat. For the Lamb which is in the midst of the throne shall feed them, and shall lead them unto living fountains of waters: and God shall wipe away all tears from their eyes."

3. *We will never suffer the agony of thirst.* But Jesus did. Those who were crucified usually died of thirst. Jesus hung there under the broiling eastern sun and cried out, "I thirst." And that request for water was denied. I have stood by the bedside of one who was critically ill. I have watched the nurse place a drop of water upon the tongue of the patient. The patient would cry out for water but it was not safe to give more than a drop or two. Suffering from thirst is an awful thing.

The sinner will suffer eternally from thirst. Jesus tells us about the rich man who went down to hell. He cried out, "Send Lazarus, that he may dip the tip of his finger in water, and cool my tongue; for I am tormented in this flame" (Luke 16:24). But a Christian will never suffer like that. Daily we are refreshed by the Water of Life, and we will never suffer the agony of thirst in eternity, all because of Calvary.

4. *We will never suffer the agony of darkness.* But Jesus did. From noon until three o'clock he hung on the cross in darkness. That darkness was symbolic of the darkness of hell. And Jesus suffered all of hell as He hung on the cross.

Now Jesus suffered darkness that we might walk in the light. I love the light. I love to wake up in the morning and see the golden sunlight bursting over the horizon. Light is always more welcome than darkness. So in heaven we are going to have eternal light. We won't need the sun or the moon. Heaven will be illuminated with the light of God's glory, and we will bask in that light forever, all because of Calvary.

5. *We will never suffer the agony of loneliness.* But Jesus did. Not one of His disciples, not one of those He had healed, not one of those He had blessed was close enough to comfort Him as He hung on the cross. It will be the same way with

the sinner in hell. Many others will be there, but none to comfort, none to console, none to offer help, none to enjoy fellowship with.

But Jesus was lonely that we might never be lonely, that we might enjoy fellowship on earth and in heaven. No, we will never be lonely in eternity, all because of Calvary.

6. *We will never suffer the agony of pain.* But Jesus did. No one has been able to fully describe the anguish and suffering He endured on the cross. Put yourself in His place. Spread your arms out. Feel the nails go through your hands and then through your feet. Then feel the excruciating pain as the cross is lifted into the air and dropped in the deep hole. Then every muscle is strained and the tendons and the flesh are torn. Feel the awful thirst, the trickle of blood running down the crown of thorns into the mouth and nose. Feel the heat of six long hours under the hot sun.

This is the picture of the sinner suffering in hell, not for six hours but forever and ever. There is only one way to escape it and that is through faith in Him who died on the cross. But because of Calvary the Christian will never suffer like that. As far as we are concerned the door of hell is forever shut when we come to Christ and God writes our names down in the Lamb's Book of Life.

So as I look upon Calvary, as I see Him dying there for me, when I realize all He has done for me, I can never be the same again. I want to spend the rest of my life serving Him. How do you feel?

Oh, I tell you, it means everything to be a Christian. So I would say, "Thank God for Calvary and Jesus and what He did for us there. Let's never forget it. Let's live for Him as long as He gives us breath."

# 7.

# The Greatest Sinner
# in the New Testament

Luke 22:54-62

Who was the greatest sinner in the New Testament? It was not Herod, although he did some awful things. When he heard that Christ had been born, he killed all the babies under two years of age in the vicinity of Bethlehem. Can you imagine the sorrow he caused? Here in a little home is a couple with a tiny baby. They love that baby with all their hearts. Then some cruel soldiers come in, seize the baby, throw it against the wall and dash its brains out. That scene was multiplied many times. Herod was cold and cruel, but he wasn't the greatest sinner in the New Testament.

Pilate was not the greatest sinner in the New Testament. He was a cheap politician. He knew Jesus was innocent and he could have freed Him. But he had his political ear to the ground, he wanted the favor of the people. So he delivered Jesus to be crucified. Yet I would not call him the greatest sinner in the New Testament.

Judas was not the greatest sinner in the New Testament. His heart was never right. He traveled with Jesus, but he was never redeemed. He betrayed Jesus for thirty pieces of silver, then in bitter remorse he went out and committed suicide. Yet I would not call him the greatest sinner in the New Testament.

The prodigal son was not the greatest sinner in the New Testament. He left his father's house and went down into an awful life of ruinous sin. Yet I would not call him the greatest sinner in the New Testament.

I make bold to say that Simon Peter was the greatest sinner in the New Testament. Why do I say that? Because his sin was against love. His sin was against the One who had done more for him than any man on earth. His sin was just opposite to all he professed to be and do. In my book, *Simple Sermons for Times Like These*, I have a sermon on "The Greatest Sinner in the Old Testament." That was David, "a man after God's own heart." By a strange coincidence we find that the greatest sinner in the New Testament was also a man very close to the Lord. We don't expect much from a man who is far from Christ, but when a child of God sins grievously, his sin is greater. So I say that Simon Peter was the greatest sinner in the New Testament.

There was nothing dull about Peter. He was often on the mountaintop and often in the valley. Sometimes we think he was the greatest saint on earth and at other times we think he was the most ungrateful sinner. He was always colorful and always interesting. He seems more human than any other Bible character. As we read the story of his life we say, "Peter was a man like the rest of us. We, too, live an up-and-down existence." When we meet Peter in heaven we will say, "Peter, we read about you in the Bible. We traveled the same road you did." Then he will say, "Yes, but the great Saviour brought us through it all and home at last, didn't He?"

Now let us look at some of the high points in the life of Peter.

    I.   His Conversion to Christ
   II.   His Call to Service
  III.   His Contacts With Jesus
  IV.   His Commission of a Great Sin
   V.   His Consecration in Later Life

## I. His Conversion to Christ

Peter was a fisherman, a commercial fisherman. He caught fish to sell and make a living, and not as a sport. Like many men who work on the sea, he was a big, rough, cursing man. He had a brother, Andrew, who was just his opposite. He was a quiet, retiring sort of fellow. We never hear him preaching great 'sermons like Peter did, but he did for Peter the greatest thing any person can do for another.

One day a rugged country preacher named John the Baptist was preaching near the home of Peter and Andrew. Peter was not interested, but Andrew went to hear John preach. While John was preaching Jesus came along. John cried out, "Behold the Lamb of God, which taketh away the sin of the world" (John 1:29). We don't know all that transpired between Andrew and Jesus, but we do know that Andrew found the Messiah and trusted Him as his Saviour.

Now let us watch Andrew. We are always eager to see what a new convert will do. Well, he ran home as fast as he could. When he found Simon he burst out with the marvelous news, "Oh, brother Simon, I have found Christ, the long-promised Messiah." Then we read these marvelous words, "And he brought him to Jesus" (John 1:42). This is indeed the greatest thing one man can do for another.

Some of the members of my church in El Paso went out one night to see a couple who were not Christians. This couple at first thought these people were selling something and would not let them in. But finally they did get in. They talked and prayed with this couple and led them to Christ. Now they are happy Christians and useful, active church members. Some day in heaven they will thank these friends for coming out and telling them about Jesus.

When Andrew led Simon Peter to Jesus, he had no idea that one day Peter would preach to a great crowd and see three thousand people saved. And you and I never know what great usefulness may be in store for someone whom we lead to Christ. A Scottish preacher, in reporting to his church officials, sadly said: "We have had only one conversion, wee Bobby Moffatt." Ah, but Bobby Moffatt became one of the greatest missionaries of all time. The men who led Spurgeon and Moody and Truett and Billy Graham to Jesus didn't realize what these men would mean to the world, but God has a way of making great things out of small.

When Jesus met Simon He said: "Your name has been Simon, from now on it will be Cephas, a stone." Now a stone is a solid thing and Peter was anything but that, but Jesus saw what he would become and named him rightly. Jesus looks upon us, not simply as we are, but as to what we might become if we surrender to the divine plan.

## II. His Call to Service

After his conversion it is probable that Peter didn't see Jesus for some days. But I am sure that his mind was full of this wonderful man. I am sure also that he was a different man. Those who fished with him must have said, "Have you noticed how different Simon is since he met Jesus? He is not boisterous and profane like he used to be." Oh, friends, if you are not different from what you used to be, you haven't met the Christ I know. "If any man be in Christ, he is a new creature: old things are passed away; behold, all things are become new" (II Corinthians 5:17).

Well, one day Peter took a day off to mend his fishing nets. And suddenly, as he busied himself about this work, a shadow fell across him and he looked up to see Jesus standing there. "You've been fishing for fish, Peter," the Master said, "follow me, and I will make you fishers of men" (Matthew 4:19). And immediately Peter, along with Andrew, left their nets and followed Jesus. Now this decision led to hardship and death, but if they had not made it, if they had stuck to their nets, we never would have heard of them.

Today men hesitate when God calls. "I am not prepared," some say. Moses said that. But I can testify that God will help you to become prepared if you will make a full surrender to Him. "Lord, I have a family to support," some say. But God will take care of that family if you take care of His work. "Lord, I have a business to look after," others say. But God calls you to a bigger business, one that pays bigger dividends than any other business on earth.

What is Christianity? It is leaving something and following Someone. It is leaving sin and following the Saviour. Christianity is not just a negative attitude of quitting something. It is a positive act of following Someone and that Someone is Jesus. Be it said to Peter's credit, he left all and followed Jesus.

### III. His Contacts With Jesus

Peter had the glorious privilege of walking with Jesus for more than three years. One night when he and the other disciples were in a ship on the sea, a mighty storm arose very suddenly. They thought they would go down at any minute. Then suddenly they saw Jesus walking on the water. They thought he was a ghost, but impulsive Peter cried out, "Lord, if that is You, bid me walk on the water" (Matthew 14:28). Now this was an impossibility. Whoever heard of a man walking on the water? But Jesus said, "Come on." And Peter stepped out of the boat and walked toward Jesus.

As long as Peter kept his eyes on Jesus, he was perfectly safe. Then maybe one of the other disciples said, "Look out, Peter, there comes a big wave." And Peter took his eyes off Jesus, looked down at the water and began to sink. As he went down he offered a short prayer, "Lord, save me" (Matthew 14:30). Just three words, but Jesus lifted him up and rescued him. Oh, when we are in deep trouble, we don't need to make a long speech to God. He hears even the groan of our spirits.

We notice that Peter began to sink when he took his eyes off Jesus. And when we take our eyes off Him, and look instead at the difficulties around us, we, too, begin to sink.

On another occasion Jesus said to His disciples. "Whom do ye say that I am?" And Peter gave the right answer, "Thou art the Christ, the Son of the living God." Then Jesus said, "Blessed art thou, Simon Barjona, for flesh and blood hath not revealed it unto thee, but my Father which is in heaven. And I say also unto thee, That thou art Peter, and upon this rock I will build my church; and the gates of hell shall not prevail against it" (Matthew 16:15-18). Was Jesus going to build His church on poor old vacillating Peter? Would he be the foundation stone for the church which would last throughout the ages? No, of course not. Two different Greek words for rock are used here. The one used for "Peter" meant a small pebble. The other word meant a mighty boulder, a great Gibraltar. Jesus was going to build His church on Himself, on the foundation fact that He was the Son of God.

On another day Jesus took Peter, James and John to the top of a mountain. There Jesus was transformed and transfigured. God clothed Him with the glory we shall behold when we see Him in heaven. And Moses and Elijah came down from heaven and talked to Jesus about the death He would soon die for sinners. The disciples fell upon their faces in fear. Finally, when they looked up, no one was there but Jesus. And Peter was so moved that he said, "Lord, let's build three tabernacles here, one for you, one for Moses and one for Elijah." Then God from heaven spoke, "This is my beloved Son, in whom I am well pleased; hear ye him" (Matthew 17:5, 6). It is not Moses or Elijah or anyone else who has life's greatest message for us. It is Jesus, Jesus only.

## IV. His Commission of a Great Sin

One day Jesus said, "My enemies are going to arrest Me and put Me to death." Immediately Peter jumped to his feet, "No, Lord, no," he cried, "they can't do that to You. They'll have to kill me before they touch You." It's mighty easy for us to talk big when the sun is shining, but it's a different matter when a shadow falls across our pathway. So Jesus looked sadly into Peter's eyes and said very gently, "Peter, before the cock crows at dawn, you will deny Me three times" (Matthew 26:34). And I imagine that Peter mumbled under his breath, "I'll show Him how strong I am. Nothing in the world would cause me to deny Him."

Well, Jesus took Peter and James and John into the garden of Gethsemane that night and these three went to sleep while Jesus prayed in great agony of spirit. Then, as they left the garden, Judas planted the kiss of betrayal on Jesus' cheek and His enemies arrested Him. Where is Peter now? Is he there standing between Christ and His enemies? No, he is following Him "afar off." That dark night Jesus was beaten and ridiculed and hurried from one trial to another. It was a cold night, so Peter came into the courtyard and warmed himself by the enemies' fire.

Suddenly a little serving maid came up to him and said, "Aren't you a follower of this Nazarene?" And Peter said, "No, no, I don't know what you are talking about." Peter thought he might get into trouble, so he slipped around to the porch. Then another maid said, "This fellow was with Jesus." And Peter ripped out a big oath and said, "I do not know the man." Then a man came up to him and said, "You are one of His. You have the same Galilean accent." And Peter began to curse and swear. "Man, I tell you," he shouted, "I don't know the man."

As soon as Peter had said that a noise floated out upon the night air. A rooster began to crow. Then Peter remembered what Jesus had said. He must have thought, "Oh, what have I done?" Soon Jesus was led by and He looked at Peter. What was in that look? It was a look of disappointment, yet it was a look of mercy and love and forgiveness. And now poor old Peter's heart just breaks. He rushed away from the crowd, found a quiet place and wept over his sin (See Luke 22:54-62). Did you ever see a strong man weep? It's a heartbreaking thing. So look at Peter and remember how he sinned against great love.

Dear friend, Peter was not the last one to commit such a sin. Jesus has loved us and done great and good things for us, yet we have often denied Him as grievously as Peter did. We deny Him by the sins we commit. We deny Him by showing the Satanic spirit instead of the Christlike spirit. We deny Him by putting other things before Him. We deny Him by giving way to our own comfort and convenience and neglecting His church and His work. We deny Him by taking the material things He gives us and using them for ourselves instead of for His glory.

Yes, we have denied Him in a thousand ways. Oh, that we might find some spot where we, too, could weep our eyes out over the way we have treated the Best Friend man ever had.

## V. His Consecration in Later Life

Jesus died the next day while Peter looked on, a broken and beaten man. Is that the end of the story? No, thank God! . . . The story of God's children does not end in defeat. For three days Peter wept and wondered. Did Jesus still love him?

Had Jesus forgiven him? Did Jesus have any future plans for him? On Sunday morning Jesus rose from the grave. And His first thought was of Peter. He sent him a message. "Go and tell My disciples and Peter to meet Me in Galilee." He didn't want Peter to feel left out, so He mentioned his name specifically. Oh, how that message must have gladdened Peter's heart!

Sometime later Jesus met the disciples by the seaside at dawn. He spoke especially to Peter. Three times he had denied Jesus, so three times Jesus asked him, "Do you love Me, Peter?" And Peter said, "Lord, You know all things. You know my heart. You know how sorry I am that I denied You. You know how miserable I've been. You know I love You." And Jesus said, "Go and feed My sheep. Preach My Gospel. Tell men what I've done for them. Serve Me until you die." (See John 21:15-17.)

Did Peter do that? I'll say he did. Fifty days later a great crowd gathered at Jerusalem. The Holy Spirit came in power upon Peter and the other disciples. He preached a great sermon and three thousand souls were saved. After that, filled with a great love for Christ and a burning missionary zeal, he went out to preach and witness and suffer for Christ. Tradition tells us that when they were going to crucify him, he said, "I am not worthy to be crucified as my Lord was, let me be crucified head downward." And as we see him dying there, we know that the man who sinned so greatly against love, now loves enough to give his life away for Christ.

And surely, when Peter reached heaven, he and Jesus had a wonderful reunion. They forgot all about the denial and the crowing of the cock and just remembered how much they loved one another.

Yes, Peter sinned against love, even though he was a child of God. Haven't we often done the same thing? Haven't we often displeased the Saviour who died for us? Yes, but as Christ loved Peter and forgave him and made him over, so will He do the same for us. We have only to come to Him confessing our sins and turning away from them. Then we will feel His loving arms around us and hear His sweet voice saying, "I forgive you, My child, go and do better now."

Ian McLaren tells the story of Jamie Sauter in one of his

books. When Jamie lay dying the preacher came to see him. Jamie said to him, "I have a bit of crepe on my hat. Will you take it and burn it? I am going to a place where they don't wear crepe. Then take my Bible and place it in my casket. It's the only thing I want to take over Jordan with me. Forty-four years ago I loved a girl and she loved me. We met often where the primroses bloomed by the stile in the field. One evening I went to meet her and she did not come. Anguish filled my soul. I went again and saw her brother approaching and I knew something was wrong. He came to tell me that she was dead. I have worn that crepe on my hat ever since and the Bible is the one she gave me."

Then the preacher said that a wonderful light filled Jamie's face. He seemed to see the lovely girl he had lost forty-four years before. He held out his hands and said, "Mamie, I have been faithful to you all these years." Then he went out to meet her. Someday you and I, by God's grace, are going out to see the Saviour who loved us and died for us. May we be able to say as we clasp the nail-pierced hands, "Dear Lord, I have been faithful to You."

# 8.

# The Friend of God

James 2:23

The poorest man on earth is the one who has no friends. I would hate to be forced to say, "I don't have a friend in the world." Friendship is a beautiful and blessed thing. When you find a true friend, you find a pearl of great price. Someone asked a great author for the secret of his success and he replied, "I had a friend." Many of us can say the same thing. We climb the ladder to success and happiness on the love and prayers of our friends.

But what is a friend? He is one who knows all about you and still loves you. He is the one who comes in when all others go out. Friendship is a matter of one soul dwelling in two bodies. David and Jonathan were great friends. When Jonathan's father sought to kill David, Jonathan helped his friend to escape. Ruth and Naomi were great friends, they shared sorrows and joys together. Damon and Pythias were such devoted friends that they were willing to die for each other. But Jesus Christ is the greatest Friend of all. "Greater love hath no man than this, that a man lay down his life for his friends" (John 15:13).

Now Abraham, in our text, was called, "the friend of God." What a wonderful title! And the beautiful thing about it is that every one of us can be friends of God, the greatest Friend.

## I. A Friend of God Has Been Redeemed

An unsaved person is a stranger to God. The Bible teaches us that he is at enmity with God. Jesus said that sinners were the children of the devil, but when we forsake our sin and trust Christ as our Saviour, we become the friends of God.

73

Mr. William Fleming of Fort Worth was a great Christian layman. When he was elected as president of the Texas Baptist Convention, Bill Marshall and I were elected as the two vice-presidents. Just as soon as the convention was over Mr. Fleming invited us to his hotel room. There we went down upon our knees and asked God to bless our efforts for Him. Mr. Fleming was a wealthy oil man who gave millions to the cause of Christ. It was said that he never let a man leave his office without talking to that man about Christ and urging him to accept Him as Saviour. Mr. Fleming started out as a poor man, but he became rich. However, rich or poor, he was a friend of God simply because he left the ranks of lost sinners and came over to the side of the Lord.

But you don't have to be rich to become the friend of God. Any man, woman or child, who comes to God as a lost sinner, trusts Christ as his personal Saviour, confesses Him publicly before the world and strives to please Him in all things day by day, becomes a child of God.

Years ago I held a meeting in Waycross, Georgia. On Thursday night, at the close of the service, a young man came up to me and said that he wanted to talk to me. I could see that he was upset. He was under deep conviction for sin. I took him into one of the Sunday school rooms. He fell down by a chair and began to sob. In a few minutes I had shown him the way of everlasting life and he was gloriously saved. . . . One week later he came to me and asked, "Do you know what night this is?" "Yes," I answered, "it's Thursday night, what about it?" And he said, "I am twenty-four years of age. I have been a Christian only one week. But I want to tell you that I've had more happiness packed into my life in this one week than in all the twenty-four years of my life." He had been redeemed, he had become a friend of God. A friend of God is one who has been redeemed by the blood of the Lamb.

## II. A Friend of God Reads the Love Letter God Writes Him

Here is a young woman who is engaged to a service man. She loves him very deeply. Soon he is sent overseas, but they plan to be married when he returns. Every morning she looks for the postman. It seems that he is always late. But he finally reaches her house and hands her a letter from her sweetheart. She takes the letter and lays it on the table and goes about her business. Her mother asks, "Is that a letter from John?" "Yes," she replies. "When are you going to read it?" her mother asks. "Oh, some other time," replies the daughter, "I have some phone calls to make now." That night she goes to a party. The unopened letter is still lying there on the table. Her mother again asks, "Aren't you ever going to read that letter?" "Oh," says the daughter, "I'll read it some day when I have nothing else to do." Now you know that isn't the way things happen. As soon as the postman hands her that letter she tears it open and reads it quickly. Then she reads it over again, slowly this time. Then she reads it over and over until she almost knows it by heart.

Well, the Bible is God's letter to you and me. How do you treat it? Do you neglect it? Do you let it lie on the table, gathering dust? It is full of good things God has put there to bless you. Don't let those blessings go unclaimed.

Now the Bible is food for our souls. The soul needs spiritual nourishment, just as the body needs physical nourishment. You can't nourish the soul on the daily newspaper or the things you find on the newstand. You need to feed upon the Bread of Life. A baby does not begin on T-bone steaks. First, there is milk, then later a stronger diet. So I would advise a young Christian to begin by reading the wonderful story of Jesus as given in the gospels. Drink the milk of the Word first. As you grow in grace and the knowledge of His Word, you'll soon be eating the meat of the great Bible doctrines.

The Bible is also a weapon. It is called "the sword of the Spirit." You need this weapon in your warfare against Satan. When Jesus was tempted He picked up the sword and drove the devil back. The psalmist said, "Thy Word have I hid in mine heart, that I might not sin against thee" (Psalm 119:11). The Christian overcomes by learning the Word of God. No man ever grew as a Christian who didn't have some knowledge of the Bible. Make the reading of it a daily habit.

### III. A Friend of God Talks to God

This means prayer. In order to get along, friends must communicate. They do that by talking to each other, but sometimes they communicate by just sitting near each other, not saying a word. That is fellowship in spirit. So there are times when we go to our knees and talk to God. There are other times when we sit before Him in silent meditation and our spirit communes with His Spirit.

In a certain village there lived a godly man whose wife had just died. He was left with three sons and he cried to God for His help in bringing the boys up in the right way. In the house there was one rush-bottomed chair beside which he often knelt in prayer. Each night he gathered his little family together in a circle around that chair and prayed for them as earnestly as he could. But the boys grew up without Christ, moved to the city and were prosperous. The good father continued to pray for them each night by the same old chair.

Then he became quite ill and soon was nearing the end. He said to a friend, "I am praying that my death will bring my boys to Christ." When he passed away, the three sons came home for the funeral. After the funeral the question arose as to what should be done with the furniture. One of the sons said, "It is not valuable, let's give it away." But the oldest son said, "I would like to have the old rush-bottomed chair. I remember how father used to pray as he knelt beside it. I have never heard such prayers. I can almost hear them now. I am going to answer those prayers. I am going to be a Christian and try to live as he did." The other two sons' hearts were softened as the Spirit of God fell upon them. They knelt with the oldest brother by the chair, gave their hearts to Christ and went out to live for Him. Oh, that we might learn the secret of prayer and the power of prayer.

Sometimes we have a close friend whom we love very much. Every day we have some contact and fellowship with him. We visit together, talk together, eat together. Then one day he tells us that he is being transferred to another city. It breaks our hearts. We say, "We must keep in touch with each other." At first we write each other regularly, we phone each other from time to time. After a few months we don't write as often and we never phone. In a few more months communication ceases and the friendship cools off. Alas, too many people treat God the same way. When they are first saved they keep in constant touch with Him. Each day they turn to Him in prayer and sweet communion. Then, as the days go by, they pray less and less until finally they almost forget Him. If you want to keep close to God as a friend, you need to keep close to Him in prayer.

## IV. A FRIEND OF GOD IS WILLING TO MAKE SACRIFICES FOR HIM

One day God decided to test Abraham's love for Him. He said, "Abraham, you have an only son. For years you prayed for this son. All your love and hopes are wrapped up in him. But I want you to go to the top of the mountain and sacrifice your son, your only son, Isaac, to me." Of course, Abraham's heart was broken. But he didn't argue with God, he didn't complain. He took Isaac to the top of the mountain and made everything ready for the sacrificial act. As he lifted the knife to plunge it into the heart of his son, God spoke from heaven, "Abraham, Abraham." And God saved the boy's life. Abraham had met the test. (See Genesis 22:1-18.) He loved God enough to give up his son for Him, even as at Calvary God loved us enough to give up His Son.

Did you ever make a sacrifice for God? Did you ever give up something you wanted desperately, in order that God might have it? William Wallace was a member of the Broadway Baptist Church of Knoxville, Tennessee, and I was his pastor. He had finished his training as a doctor. He wanted to go to China as a medical missionary. The Foreign Mission Board could not send him during the depression days of the thirties. The Board was deeply in debt and their income was so low that they could not send out any new missionaries. Dr. Wallace often spoke to me of the great dream of his heart to serve the Lord on a foreign field. In the meantime he served as house physician in the Knoxville General Hospital and awaited God's good time.

One of the Knoxville doctors offered Dr. Wallace $15,000 per year to come in with him. Now this was a lot of money in those days, but he turned the offer down, saying, "I believe God wants me to serve Him in China." After several months of taking special offerings in our church we were able to send Dr. Wallace to China. He left us on the first Sunday in September, 1935, after a great service in our church. He served in China for 15 years. He not only healed the bodies of men and women and boys and girls through his medical skill, but he won many of them to Christ through his spiritual dedication and witness. Then in 1950 the Chinese communists arrested him and put him to death. Today his body lies in a grave in far-away Red China, awaiting the resurrection morning. God said to William Wallace, "Do you love Me?" And he replied, "Thou knowest that I love Thee." "Then," said the Lord, "give Me your life, your all." And William Wallace did just that. If you are God's friend, you are willing to make any sacrifice for Him.

Take the matter of material possessions. God does not ask you to give all you have. He asks only for a tenth. Yet some people who claim to be the friends of God will not give Him even that much. But God promises to shower His blessings upon those who rightly relate themselves to Him in the matter of their material possessions. One of my deacons said, "Pastor, you asked us to give some more money for a special cause. I gave $100, and I didn't know how I could get along without it. But I went home and there was a check for $1,000 for some research work I had done which I never dreamed I would get paid for." Every tither could give similar testimonies.

The Bible says, "Seek ye first the kingdom of God and his righteousness, and all these things shall be added unto you" (Matthew 6:33). Begin by giving God a tenth. Then watch Him pour out the blessings. A man wanted to teach his little girl to tithe. He took ten dollars in his hand and said to her, "Jesus came down from heaven. He had no nice home, no car to ride in, often no place to sleep. He went about doing good and finally He died on the cross to save us and take us to heaven. Now we ought to give Him some of this money out of gratitude. So we'll keep nine dollars for ourselves and give Jesus one dollar because we appreciate what He did for us." Suddenly the little girl burst into tears. "What's the matter?" asked her father. And she sobbed, "Is that all Jesus gets?"

He doesn't get that much from many Christians. They are willing for Jesus to do all the giving. The Bible says that "it is more blessed to give than to receive," but they say, "Receiving is good enough for me." Oh, we need a revival today that will give Christians the right concept of stewardship. The friend of God is willing to make sacrifices for Him.

## V. A FRIEND OF GOD WANTS TO HAVE FELLOWSHIP WITH GOD

We like fellowship with our friends. It is fine to go on a trip with them, to go out and eat with them, to sit around and talk with them. But the sweetest fellowship in the world is that fellowship we have with God. The trouble with so many Christians is that they don't practice the presence of God. They don't think of Him very often as a real Person, but some faraway King sitting on a throne. Jesus said, "Lo, I am with you alway" (Matthew 28:20). The poet says that He is "closer than hands and feet, and nearer than breathing." Is He real to you? Do you walk with Him every day?

Some sarcastic boys said to a devout old Christian man, "How do you know that your Christ is alive?" And he wisely answered, "I talked to Him this morning."

When Dr. Ellis Fuller was president of the Southern Baptist Seminary he took a group of Christians to the Holy Land. On a certain Saturday they said to him, "Tomorrow is Sunday. We are going to Calvary and we want you to preach to us as we linger there." He said that he couldn't sleep that night and no sermon came to his mind. He said he didn't feel equal to the task of preaching at the place where Jesus died. So he spent the night memorizing the story of the crucifixion in Matthew.

On Sunday morning they walked quietly to Calvary. No one even whispered. Everything was as quiet as death. When the time came for Dr. Fuller to speak, he opened his Bible, turned his face toward heaven and quoted the wonderful story. Then he said, "Right there is where He died, right there is where He died for you and me." Every eye was filled with tears. Then he quoted the hymn:

> When I survey the wondrous cross
> On which the Prince of Glory died,
> My richest gain I count but loss,
> And pour contempt on all my pride.
>
> Forbid it, Lord, that I should boast,
> Save in the death of Christ, my God!
> All the vain things that charm me most,
> I sacrifice them to His blood.
>
> See, from His head, His hands, His feet,
> Sorrow and love flow mingled down;
> Did e'er such love and sorrow meet,
> Or thorns compose so rich a crown?
>
> Were the whole realm of nature mine,
> That were a present far too small;
> Love so amazing, so divine,
> Demands my soul, my life, my all.

Dr. Fuller said that as they turned away from Calvary everyone felt that if they had a thousand lives, they would want to give them all for the One who died there for them. What a friend Jesus is, what a Saviour! And as our Friend we can walk with Him every day.

## VI. A Friend of God Lives Forever With Him

Paul describes in I Thessalonians how Christ will some day come for His own. Then he says, "So shall we ever be with the Lord" (I Thessalonians 4:17). There is no condemnation for those who are in Christ. There is no separation for those who are in Christ. There is only glorification for those who are in Christ.

We don't hear many messages on heaven today. Maybe it's because we are so taken up with this world. But hope is the thing that keeps us going, and the Christian possesses a hope which others do not have. He knows that it is all well with his soul. He knows that death doesn't end it all. He knows that

Christ and heaven and his loved ones are waiting for him in the land of no tears.

So let us thank God that He is not only our Father, but also our Friend. Let us walk with Him every day. Let us give our best to Him. And let us never do or say anything which would cause a break in our fellowship with Him.

# 9.

# Stranger in Paradise

Luke 23:39-45

Today I want to take you to the ancient city of Jerusalem. Great crowds have gathered from all over the country. It is time to celebrate the Feast of the Passover. The people have been having a fine time of fellowship, greeting friends and relatives they haven't seen since the year before. There have been some solemn hours as they observed the religious rites of the season.

But this morning an air of expectancy fills the crowds. Something spectacular is going to happen. Three men are going to be crucified. Most of the people have never seen such a sight, so now they are waiting to look upon this gruesome spectacle. Soon the Roman centurion goes to the prison and shouts: "Bring out the prisoners."

First, Jesus Christ is led forth, wearing a seamless robe. The soldiers look at the robe covetously, wondering which one will get it when the prisoner dies. Then two other prisoners, hardened criminals, are led out. These men were awaiting execution, so Pilate figures he might as well get rid of them as he gets rid of Jesus. As the three men are led through the crowd of jeering, hooting spectators, a herald marches before them, bearing a placard telling of their crimes. On the placards of the two thieves are the words: "Robber and murderer." On the other placard we read the simple words: "Jesus of Nazareth, King of the Jews."

As the procession moves by the governor's palace Pilate gazes at them for a minute. Then, with a puzzled look on his face, he turns away. His wife, standing by, says in saddest tones, "I am afraid you have condemned an innocent man." In a few minutes the three men are nailed upon three crosses and are hanging high above the earth, while the crowd cries out in ways that show how much they are enjoying the spectacle.

Suddenly one of the criminals turns to Jesus. He makes a simple request: "Lord, remember me when thou comest into thy kingdom." And Jesus took time out from dying to say, "Verily I say unto you, this day shalt thou be with me in Paradise" (Luke 23:42, 43). That afternoon the spirit of Christ went winging back to God, and the soul of the poor thief rose with Him, there to dwell forever because of his faith and the promise made by Jesus as they hung on the nails side by side on the crosses of Calvary.

There are three things I want you to see in this dramatic story:

I.   The Man's Situation

II.  The Man's Supplication

III. The Man's Salvation

I. The Man's Situation

1. *He was a sinner.* When life flows along smoothly a man can joke and laugh about his shortcomings. But when death stares him in the face, when he realizes that he is going to stand before God in a few minutes, it is a different matter. Many men have committed crimes and stoutly denied them over the long years. Then when they sat in the death cell, a few feet away from the electric chair and death, they made a full confession. So this man, facing death, refuses to play the hypocrite, but blurts out the fact that he was a sinner.

You probably have not sinned as this man did. You are not a thief or a murderer, but the Bible shouts out the fact that you and I and all men are sinners. We are sinners by birth and sinners by choice. We were born in sin. The evil germ that flowed in Adam's veins flows in ours. And when the time came for us to make the choices of life, we chose to sin. The world is full of all kinds of men, the rich and the poor, the good and the bad, the ignorant and the educated, the black, the white, the red, the yellow, the brown. But there is one man you will never find. You will never find a man who hasn't sinned. "All have sinned, and come short of the glory of God" (Romans 3:23).

This man even admitted that it was only right that he be punished for his sin. Not many men will admit that. They will admit that they are not perfect, but they presume upon the goodness of God and say, "In spite of all that I have done, God is a God of love and will not punish me."

What a strange conception of God many men do have! If a child is arrogant and disobedient they think it is right that he should be punished. But at the same time they think they can live any old way and treat God any old way and then expect Him to reward them with prosperity and eternal life. But this thief didn't feel that way. He knew he was a sinner, he knew he deserved nothing but death and hell. And, my friend, before you can be saved, you must come to the same conclusion.

2. *He was helpless to save himself.* Here he was, nailed to a cross. Soon he would die. Today men feel that they must do certain things to be saved, but this man could do nothing. He couldn't walk down a church aisle and openly confess Christ, he couldn't be baptized, he couldn't give any money, he couldn't render any service. He was helpless to save himself. And men today cannot save themselves. All of their works are of no value in purchasing salvation. Their righteousness is as but filthy rags in God's sight. If they expect to be saved, they must depend on an outside power to do it.

Dwight L. Moody and a Mormon leader rode an entire day on a train together. Each one tried to convert the other to his way of thinking, but all efforts were in vain on both sides. When they parted Mr. Moody said: "The difference in our beliefs is a difference in spelling. You spell your religion 'do' and I spell mine 'done.' Christ has done everything necessary to save me on Calvary's cross." Yes, it's true. Christ tasted death for every man and made salvation sure for all who believe in Him.

> 'Tis done, the great transaction's done,
> I am my Lord's and He is mine.

Picture a man in a dark dungeon where there are no open doors and no windows. He is chained to the floor in utter darkness. There is no one in a hundred miles of him. Can he be saved in that condition? Yes, he has only to use his head and his heart. The work of his hands is not necessary. He can be saved by believing God's Word and trusting God's Son.

So we see the poor thief's situation. He was a sinner and unable to save himself.

## II. The Man's Supplication

Notice his simple request, "Lord, remember me." It was a request filled with pathos and humility. Why did he make such a request? Well, in the presence of Jesus he felt his sinfulness. You can't come near Christ without feeling your own sin and your own inadequacy. One day when Jesus drew near to Peter, Peter cried out: "Depart from me, O Lord, for I am a sinful man" (Luke 5:8). When Isaiah saw the Lord high on His throne he blurted out, "I am a man of unclean lips" (Isaiah 6:5).

Now the thief looks at Jesus and sees a Man without sin. He couldn't help but feel his own sin and unworthiness. He knew he needed help. When you hold a piece of coal in your hand you know it is black. Hold it close to the light and it appears blacker. Measure yourself by other men and you may feel very good about yourself. But come up close to Jesus and you'll feel that you are the blackest sinner in all the world. That's the way the thief must have felt.

A woman came to a preacher in Chicago and said, "I have talked to one preacher after another and I can't find peace for my soul. Can you help me?" The preacher replied, "If you will answer one question, I can tell you whether I can help you or not." "What is the question?" she asked. The preacher said, "Are you conscious that you are a poor lost sinner? Do you confess that you are ruined and undone?" The woman began to sob. She said, "Oh, I ought to go to hell. I don't see how God lets me live. I have never realized before what a sinner I am." "Then," said the preacher, "I know Someone who can help you." Soon she had found peace through Christ the Saviour. So the poor thief, side by side with the spotless Son of God, realizes the difference between himself and the Saviour. He realizes that he is a sinner who desperately needs help.

Now notice the man's great faith. Jesus was dying, soon He would breathe His last breath. His body would soon hang lifeless on the cross. Can He help a poor thief? The thief believes He can and asks Jesus to remember him. Over Jesus' head was the sign, "Jesus, King of the Jews." That was the joke of the day. The idea of this Man dying on a cross being a King! But the thief believed it. He had faith that this Man would come down from the cross and mount a throne. He didn't say, "Lord, remember me *if* you come into *a* kingdom." He said, "Lord, remember me *when* thou comest into *thy* kingdom." Oh, what faith he had!

His enemies cried out in derision, "Is He a King? Then He must have a crown." And they crowned Him with a crown of thorns. "He must have a scepter," they said. And they placed a reed in His hand. "We must show Him some allegiance," they said. And they came and spat in His lovely face. "He must have a robe," they said. And they placed a purple robe about His shoulders. "We must raise our hands to Him," they said. And they slapped Him with their palms and plucked out His beard. "He must have a throne," they said. And they nailed Him to a cross. But the thief was not unbelieving. He had faith that this quiet Man was a King who would someday inherit a kingdom.

This man had head faith. He looked at the inscription and believed what it said. He believed enough in Christ's Kingship to call Him "Lord." Before a man can be saved he must have some head faith. He must believe that Christ is the Son of God who died and rose again and whose blood can wash away all sin. But head faith is not enough. You can believe all the fundamental doctrines and still go to hell.

This man had heart faith, also. He not only believed something about Jesus, he trusted Him in his heart. A person is saved by what happens on the inside. Paul told the Philippian jailer to "believe on the Lord Jesus Christ" (Acts 16:31). He was not simply to believe something about Him, he had to "believe on" Him; he had to trust Him with his whole heart. The seat of religion is not in the head, but in the heart. Those people who read many books, seeking God with the head only, will never find Him. The heart must move, the emotions must be stirred.

His faith expressed a belief in a future life. It expressed the need of his soul. He confessed that Christ was divine when he called Him, "Lord." He showed his belief in the Saviourhood of Christ. He showed his belief in Christ's kingship, "into thy kingdom." He showed that he believed in His Second Coming, "when thou comest."

His faith was a courageous faith. The crowd cried out for the death of Jesus, they considered Him an evil man. This man believed in the goodness of Christ. He defended Christ when all others had forsaken Him. Do you have that courage? Can you stand up for Christ when all around you are standing against Him? Can you speak up for Him when others berate Him and His church? Oh, we ought to be able to say, "It matters not what others do or say I am going to be loyal to Christ."

You will notice that this man didn't ask for much. He just said, "Remember me." He didn't ask for a place in heaven. He didn't ask for a crown and a throne. He didn't ask, like the sons of Zebedee, to sit on His right side or His left. He just asked to be remembered. But Christ always gives us more than we ask for. So He not only remembered this man, He also gave him a home in heaven where death and trouble and sorrow could never touch him again.

### III. The Man's Salvation

"This day shalt thou be with Me in paradise."

How was he saved? It was by faith. It was not by baptism. He was dying on a cross. He couldn't be baptized. If baptism is a part of salvation, he couldn't be saved. So we know that baptism does not save. It is a matter of obedience which comes after salvation.

Neither was he saved by church membership. All the churches in the world cannot save one soul. He never partook of the Lord's Supper. He never was confirmed. He never memorized a catechism. These things cannot save.

He was not saved by his good works. He could never take a step for the Lord. He could never lift a hand for the Lord. He could never give a penny for the Lord. He could never give a testimony for the Lord. Yet he was on the way to heaven. This proves that we are not saved by our works. The Bible teaches this so plainly when it says: "By grace are ye saved through faith; and that not of yourselves; it is the gift of God; Not of works, lest any man should boast" (Ephesians 2:8).

Now suppose the thief hadn't died on the cross. Suppose the soldiers had taken him down and restored him to his family, suppose he had lived ten more years. I believe he would have been baptized, he would have joined a church, he would have partaken of the Lord's Supper, he would have given his money, he would have testified to the saving grace of Christ. Why do I say this? Because, when a man has met Christ and been saved, he will want to do all these things. He will want to follow Christ. You say you have been saved by faith. Are you showing your faith by your works?

How long did it take Jesus to save this man? How much time does it take for Him to change us from sinners to saints? How long does it take Jesus to lift us out of Satan's family and place us in the family of God? He does it in the twinkling of an eye. You don't have to beg and weep and plead for Him to save you, His arms are wide open right now. He can save you this very minute.

Now where did Jesus take this man? He took him to paradise. Where is that? It is heaven, it is where Jesus is. As Jesus died He said, "Father, into thy hands I commend my spirit." To the thief He said, "This day shalt thou be with me in paradise." So if Jesus' spirit went to God and heaven, that's where the thief went. That is paradise.

And how long will the thief be in heaven with Jesus? He will be there forever. He will be there when we get to heaven. He will be there throughout all the endless years of eternity.

> When we've been there ten thousand years,
> Bright shining as the sun,
> We've no less days to sing God's praise
> Than when we first begun.

Romans 8:38, 39 — "For I am persuaded, that neither death, nor life, nor angels, nor principalities, nor powers, nor things present, nor things to come, Nor height, nor depth, nor any other creature, shall be able to separate us from the love of God, which is in Christ Jesus our Lord."

Now this man knew he didn't have long to live, so he did something about his soul. He didn't say, as some of you are saying: "Next week or next month or next year I'll get ready to meet God." He knew he didn't have any more time. Do you know that you'll have another week or another month or another year? No. So let me urge you to come now even as the poor thief did and put all your trust in Jesus Christ.

Ernest Hemingway was a famous author. His name was known around the world. He wrote many books, he made millions of dollars, he had friends in high places, he was married several times. But these things did not bring him peace and happiness. It takes more than "things" to satisfy a man's hunger of soul and heart. It takes Jesus Christ. Since Hemingway apparently had no relationship to Christ, he put a gun to his head and blew his brains out. A fitting inscription for his tomb would be, "What shall it profit a man, if he shall gain the whole world, and lose his own soul?" (Mark 8:36).

A Texas woman went so far down in sin that she couldn't believe God could save her. So she wrote a letter to a preacher, telling him of her sin and asking him if, in the light of these things, she could be saved. Then she came to church and with downcast eyes she asked the preacher if he had read the letter and if there was any hope for her. The preacher turned in his Bible to Isaiah 1:18 and read: "Come now, and let us reason together, saith the LORD: though your sins be as scarlet, they shall be as white as snow; though they be red like crimson, they shall be as wool." The woman went away troubled. She simply could not believe it. The next night she came to church and fairly ran to the preacher with great joy on her face. She said, "I had a dream last night. Someone held the Bible before my face and it was open at Isaiah 1:18. I read that precious promise again and then I looked up to see who held the Bible, and, oh, I saw it was Jesus and I knew He meant that verse for me." The woman was gloriously saved and became a soul-winner and servant of Christ.

Like this woman and like the dying thief you, too, can be saved even now if you will but trust the Lord Jesus Christ as your personal Saviour.

# 10.

# When God Made Haste

Luke 15:11-24

We are the most impatient people on earth. We are always in a hurry, always pushing on to something else. We never have time to sit and meditate as our forefathers did. I can remember as a boy how visitors would come to see us on Sunday afternoon and how my parents and their friends would sit and talk for hours, and I had patience enough to listen to them. We don't have much time to do that now. Friendly conversation is almost a lost art.

Someone has said that in the olden days we didn't mind waiting a week for the next train, but today we let out a squawk if we miss one section of a revolving door. Another has said that there are three words characteristic of our modern life, "hurry, worry and bury." We hurry to everything, we worry about everthing, then they bury us before our time.

But God is never in a hurry. When He made the world He took His time. He created all things, then He rested. He promised to send the Messiah, and often men cried out, "How long, O Lord, how long?" But God knew what He was doing and when to do it. So when did He send His Son? "In the fulness of time" (Galatians 4:4). Often today we look out upon the world. We see all the unrest and the turmoil and the trouble that envelops the world. And we say, "Why doesn't God do something about it?" But God knows what He is doing, He knows when to intercede. We think of the Second Coming, a time when Christ shall return to straighten out the world. And we ask, "Why doesn't He come now? Oh, Lord, why do You tarry?" But God knows His business. He will send His Son when the time is ripe. I saw a sign on a church which said, "God may be slow, but He is never late." We need to remember that.

The Bible tells us of one instance when God made haste. We find it in the story of the Prodigal Son. The boy left home, he went into a far country, he lost everything that he had. When he "came to himself," he started home. When he was a great way off his father saw him coming over the brow of the hill. With a heart full of joy he ran out to meet his boy. He threw his arms around him and kissed him. He put a ring on his finger and a robe around his shoulders. He commanded that a feast be prepared for him. Now the Father in the story is God. In fact, the whole story is not so much about the Prodigal Son as it is about a loving and forgiving Father.

Here is the truth in the story. When a sinner realizes his lost condition and starts toward God in repentance and faith, God rushes out to meet him. He throws His arms around him, saves him and gives him the best He has. And if today you will turn toward Him He will hasten to meet you and save you.

There are three things I want you to see in this story.

I. THE POWER OF SIN

II. THE POVERTY OF THE SINNER

III. THE PICTURE OF THE SAVIOUR

I. THE POWER OF SIN

Here is the boy at home, discontented and restless. He is tempted by the things he hears about the far country. He makes all of his plans to leave, even securing his portion of the inheritance from his father. Soon he is on his way. When he gets to the far country he has a fine time for a little while. Everything comes his way as long as his money holds out. But the time comes when he loses everything and is in dire need. This is a picture of many sinners. They don't want to be held down by the restraints of the Ten Commandments and the laws of God. They feel the call of sin, they enter into it, they enjoy it for a while. But soon all is gone. Misery and unhappiness is their portion.

With the exception of the love of God, nothing in the world is as powerful as sin. Sin degrades. It takes a man from a high position and pulls him down to the lowest level. Sin defiles.

It takes a clean man and makes him dirty. Sin defeats. It keeps a man from going to the top. Sin destroys. It kills everything good. Sin dooms. If a man holds on to it, it will take him down to hell.

How does sin start out in one's life? Always in a small way. A thief never steals $100,000 in his first theft. He begins by committing small acts of dishonesty. A murderer was put to death some time ago in a Maryland prison. When asked how he began his career of crime, he said it started by taking small articles from the church when he attended Sunday school. Yes, sin starts in a small way. After the first act the sinner's conscience condemns him, so he says, "I must never do that again." But he does. Soon he goes deeper and deeper into sin and thinks nothing of it. He doesn't feel badly at all.

From the Sea of Galilee to the Dead Sea there is a distance of 65 miles. But the Jordan River, which runs from the Sea of Galilee, travels a distance of 200 miles. Why is this? It is because the river has innumerable curves in it. Centuries ago, in making its bed, the stream took the line of least resistance and in that way it became a crooked, winding river. That is the way men go into sin, they take the line of least resistance. It is easy to quit coming to church, so they lose the strength they could receive there. Other people are doing certain things and it's easier to follow suit than to resist. So, in devious ways, instead of fighting the down-dragging influences of sin, they gradually give in until they are caught in its net.

Do you know how our sin looks to God? It looks to Him like leprosy looks to us. Leprosy is a loathsome, polluting, unclean thing. The hair falls from the head and the eyebrows. The nails loosen, decay and fall off. The joints of the fingers and toes shrink and fall away. The gums are absorbed and the teeth disappear. The nose, the eyes, the tongue and palate are slowly consumed. And the Bible tells us that this is the way our sin looks to God. It is a loathsome, polluting, unclean thing.

When I was a boy, once a year a balloonist came to our little town. The balloon was filled from the gas generated in a pit that he had dug. Soon the balloon was bulging out on every side, yet it did not rise up. Why? Because it was held down by sandbags on every side. When the sandbags were removed, the balloon soared up into the air. Many of us ought to rise up and live for God, but we are held down by the sandbags of sin. There is a law of gravitation in the spiritual world as there is in the physical world. Oh, may God help us to throw off our sin and soar up closer to God.

## II. THE POVERTY OF THE SINNER

We have seen how the power of sin brought the Prodigal Son down. Now let us see how poor he became. He has to take a job feeding hogs, the worst humiliation imaginable to the Jewish mind. He almost starved to death. He was ready to eat the garbage that had been thrown to the swine. That's a picture of the sinner. He may have much of this world's goods, but, spiritually, he is just as poor as this boy was, physically.

Jesus said, "What shall it profit a man, if he shall gain the whole world, and lose his own soul?" (Mark 8:36). He is certainly saying that even the world's richest man, without Christ and hope, is the poorest man on earth. You can't take it with you. And even if you could, it wouldn't help you out there.

When a rich man died the question was asked, "How much did he leave?" And the answer came back, "He left it all." You may not be rich and you may never be rich, so what is the application to you when Jesus says: "What shall it profit a man if he gains the whole world and loses his own soul?" Here it is. If you spend your life for this world only and leave Christ out, where is your profit? There is no profit for you. Only hell is waiting for you.

Here is a man who is very popular in the city. His name is known by thousands. He has a nice home, he enjoys all the necessities of life and many of its luxuries. He serves as chairman on many civic committees. He rides the crest of the wave. But God says, "You are the poorest man in the city. You will have these things only a few years, then you will die and go to a place where these things cannot help you."

I don't care how wealthy you are, how well-educated you are, how happy you are, if you don't know Jesus Christ you are the poorest man on the earth. But the Christian is rich. Look what he has waiting for him at the end of the way. He has a heavenly home where trouble and death and sickness can never touch him. He has a reunion with his loved ones who have gone on before him. He has a Saviour to reward him and give him the best things of a glorious heaven.

What does the lost man have awaiting him at the end of the way? Nothing but hell and outer darkness and separation from God and eternal suffering. Tell me, how can any man afford to turn Christ down?

### III. THE PICTURE OF THE SAVIOUR

Finally, the Prodigal Son comes to realize his hopeless and helpless condition. He begins to think of all that his father has for him at home. In deepest humility he decides that he is willing to go home and be a servant for the rest of his life. Certainly anything, he feels, would be better than staying in the pigpen. So he leaves that old smelly place and starts home. Now the journey back was not like the journey coming out. He came out riding a fine horse, wearing fine clothes, his pockets full of money. He rode out in happy anticipation of the good time he was going to have. But he goes home on foot, ragged, dirty, hungry, with just a spark of hope in his heart, hope that his father will take him in and let him be one of his hired servants.

Then one day he comes to the top of a familiar hill. He sees his home lying peacefully in the valley. In a moment he spots a familiar figure. His father has seen him and is running toward him. The son doesn't know what to expect, but when his father hugs him and kisses him and calls for the fatted calf, he knows that he is forgiven and that all is well. This is a picture of the Saviour. When you come to realize your sinful and lost condition, when you turn away from sin and turn toward Jesus, He'll rush out to greet you and save you.

The father not only forgave the boy, but he ordered a feast to be prepared for him. And not only will Christ forgive your sins, but He will fill your life with good things in this world and in the next. We often sing the song, "O happy day that fixed my choice on Thee, my Saviour and my God." Do you remember that day? Do you remember the tears? Then do you remember the joy that came to your heart? Do you remember the sweet peace that filled your soul? Do you remember the assurance that you had then as you thought that, no matter what happened, all was well with your soul? Oh, that was a happy day! And what God has done for others He can do for you, my lost friend,

> There is a spot to me more dear
> Than native vale or mountain;
> A spot to which affection's tear
> Springs grateful from its fountain.
>
> 'Tis not where kindred souls abound,
> Tho that is almost heaven —
> But where I first my Saviour found,
> And felt my sins forgiven.

Charles G. Finney was holding a meeting in Detroit. One night a man came up to him and said, "Will you go home with me and talk to me about my soul?" "Yes," replied Mr. Finney. Then another man said, "Mr. Finney, that's the meanest man in town. He runs a saloon. It would be dangerous for you to go with him." "But I promised and I will go," replied the preacher. Then he and the man walked to the man's home together. When they went into the living room, the man pulled out his pistol and laid it on the table. "I will not harm you," he said, "but that pistol has killed four men. I want to ask you if there is any hope for a man like me?"

Mr. Finney replied, "God says that 'the blood of Christ cleanseth from all sin'." "But," said the man, "I own a saloon. Many times I have let men spend their last cent with me, knowing this would cause their family to go hungry. Women have pled with me not to sell any more booze to their husbands, but I have driven them out. Is there any hope for a man like me?" And again Mr. Finney replied, "God says, 'The blood of Jesus Christ, His Son, cleanses from all sin.'" "But I run a gambling den that is as crooked as Satan," said the man. "If a man leaves the saloon with money in his pocket, we take it away from him in the gambling hall. Men have gone out from the gambling tables and have committed suicide. Is there any hope for a man like me?" And again Mr. Finney replied, "God says, 'The blood of Jesus Christ cleanses from all sin.'"

"I have one more question," the man said, "I live in a beautiful home. Some years ago I went to New York on business. I met a beautiful girl. I lied to her — I told her I was a broker. We were married. When she came here and learned what I was, it broke her heart. I have an eleven year old girl. I have gone home drunk and beaten my wife and my little girl. I have made life a hell for them. Is there any hope for me?" And Mr. Finney said, "This is a black story, but God still says, 'The blood of Jesus Christ cleanses from all sin.'" "Thank you," said the man, "I'll be at church tomorrow night."

The next morning that man went into his saloon and smashed everything to pieces. Then he went into the gambling den and tore up every device in it. Then he went home, put his arms around his wife and little girl and said, "You need not be afraid of me any more. God has given you a new husband and a new father." The next night he and his wife and daughter walked down the aisle, gave their hearts to Christ and joined the church.

You have not been as wicked as that man was, I am sure. But you need Christ. What He has done for others He can do for you. He is just waiting for you to turn toward Him in repentance and faith. Then He will rush to your side and save you.

# 11.

# The Only Thing
# That Can Straighten Out the World

## Acts 1:6-11

All of us must agree that this world is in an awful condition today. Never have things been so uncertain, so unsettled. Just a few short years ago we went through the awful conflict of a World War. That war cost millions of lives and billions of dollars. Every day since then we have been in the midst of conflict. The cold war gets hotter and hotter. The nations of earth are ready to fly at one another's throats. The battle between communism and democracy rages on every part of the globe.

We have ceased to talk about "a lasting peace" for there is no peace. We build a fifty-story building for the United Nations, we pour millions of dollars into the work of the organization. But these efforts do not solve our problems. There is strife and warfare and bloodshed on every continent. Many years ago Edward Bok offered a prize of $100,000 for the best plan for world peace. He received 22,000 so-called solutions, but not one plan has succeeded.

America is vexed, not only with troubles in Viet Nam and other places, but she is plagued with seemingly unsolvable problems at home. On every side we find sin, graft, corruption, injustice, racial strife and crimes of every kind. The days and nights are crimson with the broken laws of God and man. Liquor holds our nation in a death grip, adult sin and adultery, juvenile delinquency, every type of evil is mushrooming in city and country.

What does America need? What does our tired old world need? It needs Someone to straighten it out. Dictators fail, presidents fail, conferences fail, armies and bombs fail. We need even more than a Superman to straighten out the world, we need a Supernatural Man. And I turn to the Bible and find the solution to every problem. Jesus Christ must come back. Only He can bring order out of chaos, only He can straighten out the tangled threads of this weary world. The farther down I see the world going, the more do I realize that men cannot straighten out the world. It will take the return and reign of the Son of God to do that.

## I. The Fact of His Second Coming

The world's greatest facts are found in the world's greatest Book, the Bible. We find there the fact of God. This is the first fact, the greatest fact. We must begin with that fact. We find there the fact of sin, how it came into the world, bringing sorrow and trouble and death with it. We find there the fact of Christ. We learn there of His birth, His life, His death, His Resurrection, His Ascension. We learn there the fact of salvation, how that through repentance and faith we find everlasting life. We learn there the fact of judgment and how all men must some day stand before the Almighty. We learn there the fact of eternity, those endless ages stretching out into infinity. And we learn there another great fact, the truth of Christ's Second Coming. This is just as surely a fact, a Bible fact, as the fact of God and sin and judgment.

Go with me to Olivet. Christ has been dead, but now He lives forever. He spent forty days on the earth, then He gathered His disciples together for one last assembly. He talked to them about the work that they were to do and told them of the power they would be given to accomplish this work. Then a cloud came down and surrounded Him and suddenly He ascended into heaven on the bosom of that cloud. As He disappeared beyond the blue the disciples looked on in open-mouthed amazement. Then two men in white apparel stood by them and said, "Ye men of Galilee, why stand ye gazing up into heaven? this same Jesus, which is taken up from you into heaven, shall so come in like manner as ye have seen him go into heaven" (Acts 1:11). This verse tells us as plain as day that Christ is going to return.

His return is mentioned 318 times in the New Testament alone. Paul, the great theologian, mentions it fifty times. The Lord's Supper declares it. Every New Testament writer and preacher proclaimed it.

The Panama Canal is 4,000 miles from Washington. The day it was completed President Wilson pressed a button in the capitol, the last barrier was broken down, and the waters of the Atlantic and the waters of the Pacific rushed together. One day Christ will return and the last barrier between God and man will come down. The ocean of the life of God and the ocean of the life of His children will come together, never to be separated again.

Today we are separated from God. We see by faith and not by sight. All the barriers of physical life stand between us and Him. But when Christ comes in the air, we shall go up to be with Him forever. Later, as the Bible teaches us, He shall come all the way to the earth in glory. He is going to take over as the Supreme Ruler. He will defeat all of His enemies and ours, He will straighten out the world, He will reign as King of kings and Lord of lords.

## II. The Time of His Coming

When is He coming? No one knows the day nor the hour. One day when Jesus was having a private talk with His disciples, they asked Him when He would return. He answered, "Of that day and that hour knoweth no man, no, not the angels which are in heaven, neither the Son, but the Father" (Mark 13:32). This is the only matter upon which Jesus ever expressed ignorance. We are often asked the question, "Is this it? Is this the event which is pointing to His coming?" We never know. However, I am sure that there are many signs of His coming. It may be very near, it can't be far away.

There are three distinct views as to His coming. First, there is a-milleniallism. Those holding this view, and they are many, say that there will be no millenial period, no period of a thousand years of His reign on earth. They look upon all the

Bible references to this glorious period as figurative and not literal periods.

Then there is post-millenialism. Those who hold this view say that we are going to preach and work and make the world better, then when our works have produced a perfect age, the Lord will return and the millenial age will begin. They talk of "bringing in the kingdom." But there will be no kingdom until the King appears. This view is contrary to all the facts about us. The world is not growing better, it is growing worse. The world population is increasing faster than the Christian population. More people are being born than are being born again.

The poets have sung of a day when all would be peaceful and lovely, when all the world would be one great brotherhood and all men would love one another. But as we look at the world today, we see it moving farther and farther from that dream. We have wars to end all wars, wars to make the world safe for democracy, wars to bring a lasting peace. But this will never be true as long as sinful men are running the world. Universal peace will come only when the Prince of Peace comes back.

Then there is the pre-millenial view, a view which I believe to be true. The one who holds this view sees the world going farther and farther from God and growing worse and worse. He believes that the world will develop into such a condition that only the Almighty Christ can straighten it out. Surely we are in that condition at this moment.

The Bible tells us that Christ will first come in the air. He will then take up all of His people, His saints, both dead and living, to be with Him forever. After a period in heaven, while tribulation comes upon the earth, He will come back to the earth in glory and reign with His saints for a thousand years. He will come in mighty power. His reign will be absolute. He will usher in the world's Golden Age.

Paul, the great theologian, in plain language, tells us that in the last days there will be a great falling away from the faith. Evil men will wax worse and worse. Sin and godlessness will saturate society. Aren't we in that period now? Things are worse than ever in the religious world, the political world, the educational world, the moral world. John tells us that when Jesus comes, a godless world will be arrayed against Him. Weren't these men portraying the world we live in today?

We don't know when He is coming. The main question is — are you ready for His coming? When Woodrow Wilson was a teacher in Princeton, they said to him, "We want you to be president of the university." He answered, "I am ready." When New Jersey wanted him to be its governor, he answered, "I am ready." When America called upon him to serve as president of the country, he answered, "I am ready." When he lay upon his deathbed, his personal physician, Admiral Grayson, said, "Mr. Wilson, you are dying." And he answered, "I am ready." Why could he say that he was ready? It was not because he was a preacher's son. It was not because he was a university president or a governor or a president. It was because he was humbly trusting Jesus Christ as his Lord and Saviour. Are you ready? You're not ready unless He is your personal Saviour.

## III. WHAT WILL HIS COMING MEAN?

1. *It will be a time of reward.* Paul said: "I have fought a good fight, I have finished my course, I have kept the faith: Henceforth there is laid up for me a crown of righteousness, which the Lord, the righteous judge, shall give me at that day: and not to me only, but unto all them also that love his appearing" (II Timothy 4:7, 8). Yes, that will be a time of reward for Paul and all of us who love the Saviour.

In this old world we suffer many injustices. The wicked prosper while God's children endure many hardships. In that day they shall have their rewards. Do you feel that no one appreciates your service to God? Do not worry. Keep on giving your best for the glory of God and, verily, you shall have your reward. Keep faithful, keep true to His Word, keep serving Him. Your reward will be a rich one.

Remember the Master's word to the faithful servant, "Well done, thou good and faithful servant, . . . enter thou into the joy of thy Lord" (Matthew 25:21). Oh, if we hear these words from His lips in that day, His smile will brighten all of eternity for us. His coming will bring our reward.

2. *It will be a time of reunion.* Some years ago I was asked to conduct the funeral of a tiny baby. The baby's mother was ill and could not attend the funeral. The funeral director wheeled the little casket by the mother's bedside, that she might have a last glimpse of her darling. Then as the casket was rolled out of the room, the mother screamed, "Good-by, darling, I'll never see you again." But it is not so with those who love Christ. We shall see our loved ones again. We shall have a great reunion.

A great old Southern Methodist preacher lay upon his deathbed, waiting the call from on High. His son was pastor of a country church twenty miles away. The time came for him to ride out and fill his appointment to preach, but he was reluctant to leave his father's bedside. But the father said, "Go ahead, son, and fill your appointment. Preach the Gospel faithfully. If I slip away while you are gone, you'll know where to find me." Yes, we sadly tell our loved ones good-by, but when He comes we shall see them again.

Imagine this scene. A disastrous epidemic is raging in the city. Many people are dying every day. As a certain man comes home from work, he is troubled as he thinks of his family. They may have died during his absence. As he nears the house he notices that it is in darkness. No one comes out to meet him. He is in great distress. Then as he enters the house he finds a note on the table from his wife. "Darling," she had written, "father came for the children and me and we have gone to his home in the mountains where the disease cannot touch us. Come on up as soon as you can." Ah, death often comes and takes our loved ones away and we are left broken-hearted. But there is a note for us in the Bible. "Our Heavenly Father has taken us up to His home, where there is no sickness nor sorrow. Soon you will be coming and we will have a glorious reunion."

A little child often sang the song, "There'll be no dark valley when Jesus comes." Later when she lay dying her mother asked, "Is the valley very dark?" And the little one replied, "I don't see a valley, mother, I just see Jesus." Yes, that's the sweetest part of the reunion. We are going to see Jesus one day.

3. *It will be a time of reigning.* "If we suffer with Him here, we shall reign with Him in glory." Do you suffer here for Jesus' sake? Then remember that some day you will reign with Him and share His glory.

A woman who had had a hard time in this life said to me, "If I can just have a tiny corner in heaven I will be satisfied." But God's children are going to have more than that. They are going to reign with Jesus.

## IV. In View of His Coming, What Must We Do?

1. *We must watch.* "Watch therefore: for ye know not what hour your Lord doth come" (Matthew 24:42). Here are a young man and a young woman very much in love. Then he is transferred to another city. He says to her, "I will go to this other city. I will build a home just to your taste. Then I will come back and we will be married. Then I will take you back with me to share our new home together." What does she do while he is away? Does she forget him? Does she run around with other men? Does she live as if she did not love him? No, she is watching for his return every day. She is faithful to him. Jesus said, "I am going to prepare a place for you. Someday I will come for you and take you to that home." (See John 14:2, 3.) Are you watching for Him? Are you faithful to Him? When He comes will He find you serving Him? Or will He catch you out in the world, serving sin and Satan?

2. *We must be faithful.* When a businessman goes away for a long trip, he says to his chief employee, "Look after my business while I am away and when I return I will reward you." When he returns he checks over the records and rewards his employee. Jesus said, "My work is the biggest business on earth. I am turning it over to you. I charge you to be faithful to me and my church. Occupy until I come. When I return I expect to find you faithful." Are you faithful? Not if you are not in His church, living as you should, serving as you should, giving as you should.

D. L. Moody said, "When I remember His coming I want to work three times as hard. I look upon the world as a sinking ship. God has given me a lifeboat and said, 'Moody, save all you can.' I am doing my best." This old world indeed is a sinking vessel. Men are going down on every side. God calls on us to win some. May God help every Christian and every church to be faithful. The aim of everything we do should be to win men to the Saviour who alone can redeem.

3. *We must live purified lives.* I John 3:2, 3 — "Beloved, now are we the sons of God, and it doth not yet appear what we shall be: but we know that, when he shall appear, we shall be like him; for we shall see him as he is. And every man that hath this hope in him purifieth himself, even as he is pure."

Oh, if we are His, if we realize how He loved us and saved us and made us His children, surely we will try to live more like Him every day. A certain man was saved during a revival. It had been his habit to go to a saloon and drink a beer each day at lunch time. He kept up this practice after his conversion, thinking it was all right. Then one day as he lifted the beer stein to his lips a new thought came to him. "What if Christ should return while I am in here drinking beer." This thought sobered him so that he put down the beer stein, left that saloon never to return and never to drink again. Yes, the thought of His coming ought to purify us.

But listen to this: Luke 17:34-36: "I tell you, in that night there shall be two men in one bed; the one shall be taken, and the other shall be left. Two women shall be grinding together; the one shall be taken, and the other left. Two men shall be in the field; the one shall be taken, and the other left."

Men go on side by side through life. Outwardly we may see very little difference in them. But one day there will be a great division. When He comes those who have trusted Him will go up to be with Him forever. Those who have rejected Him will be forever doomed and damned.

The Emperor Napoleon once ordered the Royal Guard to meet him for inspection at dawn. In order to reach the place of inspection these soldiers marched until after midnight in the rain. They arrived with their uniforms wet and muddy. They spent the balance of the night cleaning up and getting ready for inspection. When they faced Napoleon at sunrise their uniforms were spotless, their bayonets glistening. The Emperor was greatly moved. He said, "I am proud of you, my soldiers. After a weary march, you stayed up all night long in order to be ready to meet your Emperor."

Oh, my friends, one day we are going to meet our Saviour. It will be a wonderful day if we are ready to meet Him. It will be a blessed day if we can hear Him say, "Well done, thou good and faithful servant." It will be marvelous to know that we will be with Him forever.

In a doctor's office I saw a sign on the wall with two simple words on it, "Perhaps Today." That Christian doctor wanted his patients to ask him what these words meant, so that he could reply, "Perhaps Jesus will come back today. Are you ready?"

As John looked into heaven from the isle of Patmos, Jesus said to him, "Behold, I come quickly." And the old saint cried out from the depths of his soul, "Even so, come Lord Jesus!" God grant that we shall all be ready when He comes.

# 12.

# The Best Is Yet to Be

John 2:1-11

One day Jesus received an invitation to a wedding. It must have read something like this: "Mr. and Mrs. Solomon Levy request your presence at the wedding of their daughter, Sylvia, to Mr. Jacob Ginsburg, on June 20th at seven o'clock in the evening, at their home, 220 Main Street in Cana of Galilee." Jesus talked the matter over with his mother and they decided to attend. Mary said: "Sylvia will make a beautiful bride." And Jesus said, "Yes, and Jacob will be a fine husband. I see him often at the synagogue." But the disciples said, "Yes, and Solomon will give a big banquet. Let's go."

So they attended the wedding, Jesus, His mother, the disciples and many other guests. After the solemn wedding ceremony, all of them sat down at the wedding supper and had a good time. But soon the wine gave out. You can rest assured that, after all the Bible says against strong wine, this was not an intoxicating drink. Well, Mary told Jesus that the wine had given out. He told the servants to fill six big pots with water, then they were to draw some of the water out and carry it to the master of ceremonies. But, lo and behold, when they dipped into the jars, they brought out, not water, but the purest, richest wine. The master of ceremonies tasted the wine, smacked his lips and said to Solomon, "Old friend, you have certainly surprised us. Usually the best wine is given out at the first, but you have indeed saved the best wine until the last."

This was what Jesus had done. This is typical of all that He does. He touches lives and makes them better. He fills hearts with joy and peace. And the longer you know Him, the sweeter He becomes. As you walk with Jesus it is always "sweeter as the years go by." And still He saves the best until the last.

Robert Browning urges, "Grow old along with me, the best is yet to be." This is true only if you are following Jesus. One day you met Him and He washed your sins away. How sweet then was that wine. Afterward you had another great experience with Him and that wine was sweeter than the first. Then there came a sorrow that broke your heart, but He comforted you and that wine was even sweeter, though your tears were bitter. After life is over here then He gives us the sweetest time of all, when we enjoy heaven with Him and our loved ones. Yes, He saves the best wine until the last. For those who know Him, the best is yet to be. So let us seek some lessons for our hearts as we look in on the wedding at Cana.

## I. Jesus Is a Social Being

Here we see Him going to a wedding and a banquet and enjoying fellowship with people. Men draw a false picture of Jesus when they paint Him as a hermit. He enjoyed life and wanted others to enjoy it. He still feels the same way. He doesn't come to take the joy out of your life. He wants you to give up only those things which hurt you.

Suppose that you are sitting at a table laden with good things to eat and drink. But one glass is filled with poison. You pick up that glass and are about to drink the poison, but a friend rushes up and knocks the glass out of your hand. He gives you another glass, saying, "Here, drink this. There was poison in the other glass and it would have killed you." You would love that man and thank him. But that's just what Jesus does. The poison of sin would damn you, but He takes it away and gives you something better in its place.

We read of priests and nuns and other ascetics who go far away by themselves, who have no communication with the world, but what contribution can such people make to the world? Men are suffering on every side, they need help. That help never comes from a cloistered retreat. We are to live by the side of life's road and be a friend to man. Jesus did not hide Himself,

He was a social being. He went where people were and ministered to their needs.

One of our poets has said, "Pale Galilean, thou hast conquered and the world has grown grey from thy breath." Oh, He was not a pale weakling. He was a ruddy, rugged, strong he-man. The world has not grown gray because of Him, but is filled with joy and happiness. He doesn't take away our joy; He brings many of us with Him.

I once knew a woman who was too religious to smile. She wore a solemn expression on her face. She was always talking about how good she was. To be around her was like attending forty funerals. Once she remarked that no one could ever say that she had done anything wrong. But her attitude was repulsive to her children. When they grew up no one could get them to come near a church. Oh, give us a happy religion! With such a great Saviour as Christ we have a right to be happy.

Yes, Jesus was a social being when He was here on the earth. He is still a loving Friend who wants to enter joyfully into every area of our lives.

## II. Jesus Is Interested in the Institution of Marriage

God looked down upon Adam in the lovely Garden of Eden and saw that he was lonely, he was not complete. He said, "It is not good that the man should be alone. I will make him an help meet" (Genesis 2:18). So God put Adam to sleep and performed the first major surgical operation. He took a rib from Adam's side and made him a companion, Eve, the first woman. She was not taken from his head, that she might rule him, neither was she taken from his foot, that he might dominate her. She was taken from his side, that she might walk with him, bearing with him all of his sorrows and enjoying with him all of his pleasures.

Jesus was never married. He had a relationship with the world that could not be marred by any fleshly relationship. Yet He put His stamp on marriage. Today, when under God, a man and woman come together in love for their hearts to be joined together in holy wedlock, Christ puts His approval on that union.

Marriage is the fitting sign and seal of love. A marriage not based upon love does not have God's approval.

Mr. Wang was a very wise Chinese judge. Two men and a woman came before him. The first man had been married to the woman but had been reported killed in the war. Later she married the second man. Then in a few months the first husband showed up. Both of the men wanted the woman. The judge asked her, "Which one was the best husband?" She replied that they were both perfect husbands. The judge then told the two men that he would keep the woman in the custody of the court for a week. At the end of that time the men were to return for the judge's decision.

When the men faced the judge one week later, he said to them, "I am sorry to tell you that the woman died during the last week. Now let the husband take her and bury her." "Oh, no," exclaimed the first husband, "not me." Then the second husband said, "I'll be glad to take her and give her the best burial possible." The judge then clapped his hands and the woman came from behind a curtain. The judge then said to the second husband, "You take her. You are the one who merits her service and her love." Yes, love makes the world go around and Jesus greatly approves of a marriage based on love.

Jesus was invited to this wedding and He ought to be invited to every wedding. A couple should begin married life with Him and walk with Him to the end. There is no finer sight on this earth than to see two people walking together in love, with Christ by their side. You can't build a real home if you leave Christ out.

### III. Jesus Is Interested in the Commonplace Things of Our Lives

He was concerned that the wine gave out. He is interested in every area of our lives, our business, our home, our education, our future security. He is simply interested in people and everything about them. After His Resurrection Jesus met His disciples on the seashore at dawn. They had been fishing all night. Jesus called to them, "Boys, have you caught anything?" They replied, "No, we haven't had a nibble all night." "Cast your net on the other side of the boat," Jesus told them. When they did so, they brought up their net loaded with fish.

Jesus had a fire ready on the beach, so He said, "Bring some of your fish and let's have breakfast together." How beautiful, how wonderful! The amazing Christ had just conquered death, but He was interested in the fishing venture of His friends. He knew they were hungry and He wanted to have breakfast with them. And He is "the same yesterday, and today and forever" (Hebrews 13:8). He is interested in everything and anything that concerns us.

## IV. JESUS CAME TO TRANSFORM LIFE

He took the plain common water and turned it into luscious wine. He transformed it. This is what He does to all of life. He lifts the lower to the higher. He makes a garden of the desert. He takes us poor human pieces of clay and makes us fit for fellowship with the angels.

Once the cactus plant was an ugly plant, ready to pierce the hand of anyone who touched it. Then Luther Burbank fell in love with the cactus. He worked with it and experimented with it until finally it was covered with flowers. But this is nothing compared to what Jesus does with hearts that are surrendered to Him.

He took a profane, blundering man like Peter and made him one of the greatest preachers in the world. He took a thunderbolt like John and made him an apostle of love. He took Levi, a grasping tax-collector and made him to be Matthew, who wrote the first gospel! He took a demon-possessed Mary Magdalene and made her the first herald of the Resurrection. He took murderous Saul and made him into Paul, the mighty missionary. And He is still in the business of transforming men.

Now Christ's work is always superior to man's work. The first wine at the feast was good, the wine Jesus made was unbelievably superior. Men try to make others over and they fail. It takes Jesus to transform life. We pass laws prohibiting certain things, but these laws are not always effective. They do not reach and change the hearts of men. But when Christ comes into a man's heart, that man will do what is right, regardless of the law.

Yes, Jesus touches and transforms all of life. The bitterest water turns into the sweetest wine at His touch. Lives are transformed by the Great Transformer.

### V.  Jesus Uses Others to Accomplish His Purposes

He could have made new wine by speaking a word, but He used other people to help Him. He called on the servants to do their part, then He was ready to do His. When He wanted to feed five thousand people, He used a little boy who had some loaves and fishes. When He wanted to cure a paralytic He used four men to bring the sick man to Him. When He wanted to raise Lazarus from the dead, He used some men to roll away the stone. When He wanted to arouse the religious world and bring religion back to Calvary, He used Martin Luther. And I could go on and on. He uses men today. When we do our part He always does His.

When a farmer wants a crop he does his part. He plows and plants and cultivates and God does the rest. The doctor examines a patient, diagnoses the case, gives medicine or performs an operation. God does the rest. Galen said, "I bind up the wounds, God does the healing." And when God wants to grow a great church He doesn't send it down out of the skies. He depends upon us to give and serve and preach and pray and witness. Then He gives the results.

Yonder is a great orchestra of seventy-five instruments. Over in the corner there is a little man who plays the piccolo. As the conductor rehearses the orchestra all the great instruments boom out in a grand concert. The piccolo player feels that he means nothing in the great crescendo, so he quits playing. Immediately the conductor stops everything and says, "Where is the piccolo?" The piccolo player finds that although he is only a small part of the great orchestra, the leader is counting on him. Maybe you feel that you are but a small part of the kingdom of God. All that you do is fill a pew and contribute your tithe. But the Master is counting on you to be faithful. He misses you when you fail to do your part.

## VI. Jesus Always Gives in Abundance

In the story of the wedding we see Him giving them one hundred and twenty gallons of wine. He does everything in a big way. Think of outer space. He spreads it out so that man can never conquer it all. He made the sun for light and heat and He made it so hot that He had to put it 93,000,000 miles away. He wanted us to enjoy the stars, so He made, not a few, but a heaven full of them. When He formed the mountains He made, not a few hills, but the Andes and the Rockies and the Himalayas and the Alps. He wanted us to enjoy the flowers so He gave us, not a few blossoms, but decked the hills and the valleys with them. For water He gave us, not a bucketful, but He scooped out the seven seas. What a God He is, indeed!

And when we come to the spiritual realm, we see Him giving greater than ever. We need redemption and we read, "With Him is plenteous redemption" (Psalm 130:7). We need pardon and we read, "Let the wicked forsake his way and return unto Me and I will abundantly pardon" (Isaiah 55:7). We need salvation and we read, "He will save unto the uttermost all who come unto Him by faith" (Hebrews 7:25). We need an answer to our prayers and we read, "Call unto me, and I will answer thee" (Jeremiah 33:3). We need life and we read, "I am come that they might have life and that they might have it more abundantly" (John 10:10). We need a heavenly home and we read, "I go to prepare a place for you, that where I am there you may be also" (John 14:3).

Solomon prayed for wisdom and God gave him more, He gave him riches and honor. He always gives us more than we ask for. He is the great Abundant Giver.

## VII. With Jesus Everything Gets Better as We Go Along

Those people at the wedding feast expected good wine at the first and poorer wine as the feast continued. But that is the devil's way. He makes things look good for us, but the end thereof is bitter and tragic. Jesus promises everything better and sweeter as we follow Him. With Him life is always climbing toward the great climax.

A blind man was dying and someone said to him, "There is one consolation, you will soon be in heaven." "Heaven," said the dying man, "I have been living in heaven all these years since I met Jesus." This is true of the genuine Christian life. It grows sweeter and better every day and reaches its climax when we meet Jesus face to face.

A man tells of going to a mountain resort hotel for his vacation. When the bellboy led the way into his room, the man went over to the window and looked out at the gorgeous mountain scenery. He said, "That is the most beautiful sight I ever looked upon. I could never grow tired of it." Then the bellboy said, "But just wait until you see the other side. You won't think this side is so beautiful. It's just one great mass of flowers over there." Oh, life may be very fine for you down here, it may be growing sweeter every day. But this life here will not compare to that life on the other side.

Proverbs 4:18 — "But the path of the righteous is as the shining light, that shineth more and more unto the perfect day."

Now here's the application of the Cana story for us. When Jesus gave the orders to the servants, Mary said, "Whatsoever he saith unto you, do it." So today we are to do what Jesus says. We are to trust Him, follow Him, love and obey Him. Then He'll turn our water into wine and make all of life sweeter for us.

In Red China a loyal Chinese Christian was persecuted by the Communists. They told him that he would have to walk through the streets and cry out, "I am a slave of the foreigners." He said, "I won't do that, but I will cry out, 'I am a slave of Jesus Christ.'" They didn't see the significance of it, so they gave him their permission. So each day he proudly walked through the streets, crying out, "I am a slave of Jesus Christ."

Oh, that we might have that spirit! Then we would know as we walk with Him that the best is yet to be.